A Practical Guide
to
Sermon Preparation

A Practical Guide to Sermon Preparation

by

Jerry Vines

MOODY PRESS

CHICAGO

Vines, Jerry.
A practical guide to sermon preparation.

Bibliography: p.
1. Preaching. I. Title.
BV4211.2.V56 1985   251'.01   85-7228
ISBN: 0-8024-6744-X

9 10 8

Printed in the United States of America

Contents

91730

Foreword

This book is a road map, a blueprint, and a trumpet call to immediate action.

It is a road map because it traces the author's pilgrimage from traditional sermons to the excitement of biblical expository preaching. I have a feeling that many ministers of the Word are on the pilgrimage now, and they need to hear the reassuring voice that Dr. Vines gives in these pages: "Brother, you can do it!"

They will also appreciate the blueprint that he shares for effective expository preaching. He has done both his homework and his heartwork, and he is not afraid to chronicle his own mistakes and frustrations. He has summarized for us the principles and procedures that govern effective expository preaching. No matter how long a man has been ministering, he ought to review these principles and procedures regularly.

One of the best things about this book is its clear trumpet-call to action! You will not be into this book very far before you catch the excitement that motivates the author's life and ministry. I cannot conceive of a minister reading these pages and not being moved by what the author has written.

I especially appreciate the emphasis on the spiritual life of the preacher. It is not enough to have a prepared message—there must also be a prepared servant to deliver the message. May God deliver us preachers from "techniques" that produce "results," when what we need is spiritual cultivation that produces fruit.

It has been my privilege to minister to hundreds of congregations in many parts of the world. It does not take long to discern what kind of appetite each congregation has. Some churches want to be entertained, whereas others want to be edified. Usually, the attitude of the congregation toward the Word is an indication of what their pastor has been doing in his pulpit ministry. A congregation with a healthy appetite, excited about the Word, is usually pastored by a man who loves the Bible, loves his people, loves to preach, and is himself excited about what God is saying from the Bible.

Dr. Vines is that kind of preacher. I ministered the Word in one of his congregations a few years ago, and I was deeply impressed with the way his people responded. It was obvious that a steady diet of expository preaching, prepared and presented by a man with a pastor's heart, was transforming the lives of the people. I came away from that conference refreshed and enriched simply because of the way the people responded to the Word.

I am glad Dr. Vines has shared himself, his experiences, and his convictions in the pages of this book. Any sincere minister who takes this book seriously cannot help but become a better person and a better preacher of the Word.

WARREN W. WIERSBE
"Back to the Bible Broadcast"
Lincoln, Nebraska

Acknowledgments

I am grateful for the assistance of many people in the preparation of this book: Dr. Paige Patterson, who urged me to begin and drove me to completion; Shirley Cannon, who prepared the manuscript; the First Baptist Church of Jacksonville, Florida, the greatest New Testament fellowship I know about, who constantly challenges me to prepare better sermons; and my wife, Janet, and our children, who love me through all the agony of writing.

Introduction

The call to preach is exactly that—a call to *preach*. My own call at age sixteen is still very real to me. I suddenly needed to get together a sermon and find someplace to preach it. Because I had been listening to sermons most of my life, I had some idea of the format a sermon should follow. I put together a simple, brief message. When the opportunity came I delivered it. The effort was meager but exhilarating and satisfying. Little did I realize the night I preached in a little country church what the years ahead would bring. Since that night I have preached hundreds of sermons; my weeks are filled with preparing and preaching. Many weeks I preach at least a sermon a day.

The call to preach is more than that, however. There is also a call to prepare. I believe God gives to those He calls the necessary gifts to preach, and He expects the man He calls to prepare himself as best he can. In one sense, that preparation involves a man's lifetime: Men prepare sermons; God prepares men. But also included is the matter of preparing sermons.

That is why I have written this book. Perhaps most of the time in any given week of a preacher's life is devoted to sermon preparation. That is certainly true for me. Most of my hours are spent preparing sermons. Because of that, I have been greatly interested in the matter of sermon preparation throughout my years of ministry.

Some preachers I have known, using Mark 13:11 as their proof text, have refrained from preparation, claiming they allow the Holy Spirit to fill them when they preach. There was a time when that sounded good to me. I was interested in avoiding as much work as possible! I made attempts on several occasions. I stood to preach, opened my mouth, and my mouth was indeed filled—with hot air!

I recently read about a preacher of this persuasion. Meeting a preacher who was studying his sermon notes, the brother declared, "I don't study to preach. I just get in the pulpit, and the Holy Spirit fills me." The preacher who was studying his sermon notes asked, "What if the Holy Spirit doesn't fill you?" The other replied, "I just mess around until He does." A lot of church congregations would lament that too much messing around is going on and not enough preaching.

Of course, sermon preparation alone does not make a man a preacher. As I have already indicated, only God can make a preacher. But a man so called can learn basic principles of effective sermon preparation. Erasmus once said, "If elephants can be trained to dance, lions to play, and leopards to hunt, surely preachers can be taught to preach." The purpose of this book is to give practical help to the man who is faced with the responsibility of preparing weekly sermons. Sermon preparation is at once the most fulfilling and frustrating experience a man can undergo. This book should help reduce the frustration and increase the fulfillment.

I am specifically interested in the preparation of expository sermons. Thousands of churchgoers throughout America are desperately hungry for good preaching. They are looking for a Bible study, a church, or some service where their souls can be fed from the Word of God. Much of the preaching of our day is dry, irrelevant, and deadening. I believe the solution is to be found in expository preaching.

Expository preaching can be one of the richest experiences the preacher ever has. We could compare it to mining a beautiful diamond. We admire the beauty of a well-cut diamond, but what if you found the diamond for yourself—dug diligently for it, cut it carefully, then polished it to a brilliant shine? Your sense of fulfillment would be even greater. That is something of the richness of expository sermon preparation.

I am writing this book from my own experience. My life and ministry were changed when I decided to devote myself to expository preaching. The first ten years of ministry, my sermons were generally topical in nature. The Lord blessed my meager efforts. My churches had some growth. People came to Christ. Then I actually stumbled upon the method of expository preaching. At a Bible conference I had the opportunity to hear Dr. Warren Wiersbe teach the Word. Although I was a seminary graduate and had been preaching for several years, I had never heard anyone take the Bible and expound it as did Dr. Wiersbe.

My approach to preaching completely changed. I determined to begin using the expository method. All I had to go by was Dr. Wiersbe's example. I had never studied the expository method, I was aware of no books on the subject, and I had heard very little preaching of that kind. I just had the conviction in my heart that that was the kind of preaching the Lord wanted me to do. So I started. My efforts at the beginning were very poor and tentative. As I went along, however, I began to notice a change in my ministry. The people started bringing their Bibles; they showed more interest. I saw growth in the spiritual lives of my people. That convinced me of the value of expository preaching. The value to my own life is beyond my ability to place on the printed page. Only eternity will reveal what the expository method of preaching has done in me. The value in the lives of the people who have heard me preach will await the evaluation of the Judgment Seat of Christ. There is little doubt in my mind that the people themselves have been blessed through the preaching of expository sermons.

In one sense this book will be a telling of my own pilgrimage through the fascinating world of sermon preparation. Writing this book has been a tremendous learning experience for me. If no one else is blessed by its composition, I certainly have been!

My desire is to be of help to my preacher brethren. God has placed a love in my heart for preachers, and I desire God's very best for them in their ministries. If this book can be used to accomplish that, I will be richly repaid. I make no claims to being an authority in the field, but through the years God has given me insights that perhaps will further the work being done in the field of expository preaching. I hope this book will stimulate others to dig even deeper and to uncover additional insights in the area of exegetical, expository sermonizing.

After the preacher has learned to put an effective expository sermon together, he must then know how to deliver that sermon.

Much of the success of an expository sermon lies in its delivery. There will be some reference to delivery in this volume, but full discussion of delivery will have to await my second volume.

I am indebted to many people who have helped me develop my own approaches to expository sermon preparation. As I have already indicated, Warren Wiersbe was extremely helpful. Other great Bible teachers in our time have challenged me. Many excellent volumes, old and recent, have given me helpful approaches to expository sermon preparation. I have been blessed by the preaching ministry of many of my contemporaries in Southern Baptist pulpits. Dr. Adrian Rogers is an expository preacher par excellence. Dr. W. A. Criswell broke the ground for all the preachers in my particular denomination. I shall be forever indebted to him. Dr. Homer Lindsay, Jr., my partner in the ministry at First Baptist Church, Jacksonville, Florida, has been a great inspiration in the area of preaching from the Bible. Dr. Paige Patterson, president of the Criswell Center for Biblical Studies, has encouraged me in the preparation of this volume. The Criswell Center is one of many schools God has raised up to help young preachers learn how to preach expository sermons. All these men and many more have been instrumental in my own growth as an expository preacher.

But enough said by way of introduction. Let us get about the task of preparing expository sermons!

I

The Expository Method Examined

There is today a renewed interest in Bible preaching. This is a healthy and hopeful trend. Many young preachers are turning to the Bible for the substance and authority of their preaching. The term *expository preaching* is heard more frequently now than in previous years. Because that is true, we need to define expository preaching and discuss the expository method of sermon preparation. My main emphasis will be upon preaching through books of the Bible, using the expository method. We will include examples of good expository preachers. This will not be an attempt to give an exhaustive discussion of men who have successfully used the expository method. Rather, I will mention various men who can serve as role models in expository sermon preparation. This chapter also contains a variety of approaches to expository preaching. Emphasis will be placed upon the advantage of using the expository sermon model in sermon preparation.

The second section of this chapter will examine the biblical roots of the expository method. If we are going to use this method, we must be convinced that it has biblical support. A careful study of Old Testament and New Testament terms that relate to preaching will be given. I will devote special attention to the methods of the Lord Jesus and the apostle Paul. Through this careful study of the Bible terms used for preaching, you will be able to understand the biblical precedent for the expository method.

Finally, this chapter includes a discussion of the advantages of the expository method. I approach this section with a biased perspective.

The advantages both to the preacher and to the people are numerous and impressive. In an effort to be fair, I do consider disadvantages and dangers that attach themselves to expository preaching.

The first sixty years of the twentieth century witnessed a dearth of good preaching in America. Many lamented the decline of good preaching in the pulpits of the land. Merrill F. Unger, writing in 1955, said, "To an alarming extent the glory is departing from the pulpit of the twentieth century."[1] I do not doubt that assessment was true. Probably even in the 1980s there is still a famine of good, solid Bible preaching throughout the land. But we are experiencing at present a resurgence of interest in and practice of good preaching. That is certainly true in my own Southern Baptist denomination. When I first began preaching in the 1950s, expository preaching was rare. Today many pastors are seriously pursuing the expository method. That may be one of the reasons our churches are experiencing solid, substantial growth. The time is right for a renewed emphasis on the expository method.

Basic Definitions

As we begin a discussion, I will summarize some basic definitions in the field of sermon preparation. First, consider the term *homiletics.* Homiletics is the art and science of saying the same thing that the text of Scripture says.[2] The study of sermon preparation is technically called homiletics. Andrew Blackwood says, "Homiletics is the science of which preaching is the art and the sermon is the finished product."[3] Homiletics is the application of general and specific principles of Bible interpretation that are necessary to understand the Bible text.

Another term is *exegesis,* coming from the Greek word *exēgēsis,* which means a narration or explanation. The noun form of the Greek word does not occur in the New Testament. The verb form *exēgeomai,* which means "to lead out of," does occur. The word is found in Luke 24:35; John 1:18; Acts 10:8; 15:12, 14; and 21:19. In John 1:18 we are told that Christ "exegeted" the Father to man. Exegesis is the

---

1. Merrill F. Unger, *Principles of Expository Preaching* (Grand Rapids: Zondervan, 1955), p. 11.
2. Walter C. Kaiser, Jr., *Toward an Exegetical Theology* (Grand Rapids: Baker, 1981), p. 193.
3. Andrew Blackwood, *The Preparation of Sermons* (Nashville: Abingdon, 1948), p. 18.

procedure one follows for discovering the intended meaning of a Bible passage. The preacher wants to adequately represent what the text of Scripture says itself. He must avoid the danger of *eisegesis,* which is reading into the text what the interpreter would like it to say.

A similar term is *hermeneutics.* The Greek word translated hermeneutics is *hermēneuō.* In half of its occurrences the word means "to translate." A related word, *diermēneuō,* means "to expound" or "to interpret." Hermeneutics may be defined as the science of expounding or interpreting what a passage of Scripture says.

The word *sermon* refers to the product of the processes of homiletics, exegesis, and hermeneutics. The message given by the preacher to the people results from his own investigation and organization of the Bible text.

KINDS OF SERMONS

As we move toward a definition of the expository sermon, a brief discussion of several other types is necessary. The *topical sermon* is built around some particular subject or idea. That idea may be taken from the Bible or from outside the Bible. As we shall see, a topical sermon may be presented in an expository manner. Doctrinal sermons easily lend themselves to this approach. But usually the preacher gathers what the Bible teaches about some particular topic, organizes the passages into a logical presentation, and then delivers a topical sermon. However, in my opinion, it is one of the poorest ways to preach. Walter C. Kaiser, Jr., says the preacher should preach a topical sermon only once every five years, and then immediately repent and ask God's forgiveness!

A *textual sermon* is one based on a verse or two from the Bible. The main theme and the major divisions of the sermon come from the text itself. This sermon seeks to expound what the text itself actually says. Some of Charles H. Spurgeon's greatest messages are built around a single verse of Scripture.

Textual preaching has some serious shortcomings. The preacher may practice imposition, not exposition. He may choose a text as a mere starting point from which to express an idea he is fond of. Or, he may use a text as a peg on which to hang something he would like to say. Very often a text is made to serve the preacher's intentions rather than those of God's Word.

The *ethical discourse* is taken from a specific Bible passage that directs an ethical message to the believer. The purpose of the sermon is to build Bible morality into the members of the congregation. We recognize that the majority of the Bible is written to the believer. It stands to reason, therefore, that the great bulk of the preacher's sermonic efforts will be in the direction of the Christian believer. This particular kind of sermon may or may not be expository in nature. Expository preaching, correctly done, should have strong ethical and moral content. The epistles of Paul cannot be accurately expounded without dealing with the great ethical issues our people face.

One of the poorest methods is what is commonly called the *allegorical*. This sermon takes certain Bible narratives and gives them an allegorical interpretation. Such a sermon could be preached from the parable of the Good Samaritan. The preacher would explain the man on the road to Jericho as a lost sinner; the priests and the Levites would represent the efforts of the law to save him; and Jesus would be the Good Samaritan. Although all of those truths are indeed biblical, the allegorical method does violence to the literal intention of the Bible narratives.

A very popular and effective sermon is the *biographical*. This sermon presents a study of the life of a particular Bible character. The facts about the particular character form the basis for a message that has modern application. Very often God has a way of teaching truth by wrapping it in flesh and blood. The truth of faith is clearly seen in the life of Abraham, the father of the faithful. The danger of carnality is graphically portrayed in the life of Lot. The biographical sermon can be handled in an expository manner.

A more recently popular sermon is the *dramatic monologue*. In this sermon the preacher becomes the character he is seeking to present. In the pulpit he acts out the message of the character. Many times the preacher will dress himself in authentic Bible attire. This has become an increasingly popular method of presenting sermons. Done well, dramatic monologue may be very effective.

Something can be said for most of these kinds of sermons. Each one certainly has its strong point. For me, however, the expository method of preaching has become the best. The expository sermon feeds my own heart, and the people to whom I preach seem to be more blessed by expository sermons.

THE EXPOSITORY SERMON

If we are going to use the expository method, we must certainly know what it is. It is interesting that there has been a great difference of opinion and not a little confusion about exactly what constitutes expository preaching. Some believe expository preaching is making a few remarks based upon a long passage of Scripture. That misunderstanding caused the method to fall into disrepute in earlier years. There is probably nothing so dull and wearisome as that approach to preaching. A preacher using this method was once giving a long, laborious series of lectures on the minor prophets. After many, many weeks he finally came to the book of Amos. "We have now come to Amos," he said. "What shall we do with him?" A man near the back of the church said, loud enough to be heard by all, "He can have my seat, for I'm going home."[4]

Others define expository preaching as giving a sermon from a Bible passage of many verses. Andrew Blackwood says that an expository sermon is based upon "a Bible passage longer than two or three consecutive verses."[5] He believes an expository sermon differs from a textual sermon primarily in the length of the Bible passage.

Still others approach expository preaching as an exhaustive and exhausting report of all the commentaries a preacher has read on a particular passage of Scripture. That, too, can be most boring; God have mercy on any congregation that is subjected Sunday by Sunday to a report of the preacher's reading for the previous week.

Some have understood an expository sermon to be a lifeless, meaningless, pointless recounting of a Bible story. I can still remember hearing a very fine man deliver such a sermon from John 10. He told us all the particular details about a sheepfold. We were given a complete explanation of the characteristics of sheep. We were informed about the methods of an Oriental shepherd. When the message was ended, we were still on the shepherd fields of Israel. We knew absolutely nothing about what John 10 had to say to the needs of our lives today. That is not expository preaching.

Expository preaching is discredited in many places not because the method is poor, but because it is poorly used. If we are going to

4. F. B. Meyer, *Expository Preaching* (Grand Rapids: Baker, 1974), p. 30.
5. Andrew Blackwood, *Preaching from the Bible* (New York: Abingdon, 1941), p. 38.

use the expository method, let us be sure we take the proper approach.

None of those definitions adequately convey the meaning of the expository method. An expository sermon is not determined merely by the length of the passage considered. A sermon is expository by the *manner of treatment* of the passage. This is the vital meaning of exposition: An expository sermon makes plain what the Bible passage says and gives good application to the lives of the hearers. Expository preaching is not merely preaching about the Bible but preaching what the Bible itself says.

Perhaps the definitions of several others will be helpful. Donald Grey Barnhouse says, "Expository preaching is the art of explaining the text of the Word of God, using all the experiences of life and learning to illuminate the exposition."[6] G. Campbell Morgan says, "Being sure that our text is in the Bible, we proceed to find out its actual meaning, and then to elaborate its message. The text has postulates, implicates, deductions, application."[7]

The expository preacher's main concern is to set forth the truth of God's revelation in language that can be understood. The true Bible expositor will "deliver the goods to the door" of men's daily needs. He will learn by the help of God to so present and apply Bible truth that it actually becomes the living Word of God to his hearers. The passage of Scripture will provide the ideas for the message. He will take the passage apart to analyze its contents, which he will examine from every possible angle. The passage will be squeezed and made to yield all its rich treasure.

Ephesians 4:11 makes clear that the pastor is to be a pastor-teacher. To be faithful to his high calling the pastor must teach the Word of God to his people. The faithful pastor will make a serious and sincere attempt to unfold the actual grammatical, historical, contextual, and theological meaning of a passage. He will then seek to make the meaning of that passage relevant to the lives of his hearers. To do that he will properly organize, adequately illustrate, and forcibly apply its message.

For a sermon to be expository the following must take place: The sermon must be based upon a passage from the Bible. The actual

---

6. In Farris D. Whitesell, *Power in Expository Preaching* (Old Tappan, N.J.: Revell, 1963), p. XI.
7. Ibid., p. XII.

meaning of the Bible passage must be found. The meaning of the Bible passage must be related to the immediate and general context of the passage. The eternal, timeless truths in the passage must be elucidated. Those truths must be gathered around a compelling theme. The main points of the sermon must be drawn from the Scripture verses themselves. Every possible method to apply the truths found in the verse must be utilized. The hearers will be called to obey those truths and to live them out in daily life. Jeff Ray summarizes the expository method well when he says: "In preaching, exposition is the detailed interpretation, logical amplification, and practical application of Scripture."[8] My formal definition of an expository sermon is as follows: *An expository sermon is one that expounds a passage of Scripture, organizes it around a central theme and main points, and then decisively applies its message to the listeners.*

EXPOSITORY PREACHING

When I refer to expository preaching I mean to take a book of the Bible, divide it into paragraphs, and consecutively preach from them. William M. Taylor defines expository preaching as "the consecutive interpretation and practical enforcement of a book of the Bible."[9] Andrew Blackwood understands the expository sermon in that manner as well. He encourages preaching from paragraphs of Bible books, although he counsels to use the method sparingly, to give people an opportunity "to become accustomed to this novel sort of diet."[10] This method is preeminently the best method. The best preaching a man can do is to go through the books of the Bible, book by book, paragraph by paragraph, in a systematic fashion. F. B. Meyer heartily recommends the expository method. He defines expository preaching as "the consecutive treatment of some book or extended portion of Scripture on which the preacher has concentrated head and heart, brain and brawn, over which he has thought and wept and prayed, until it has yielded up its inner secret, and the spirit has passed into his spirit."[11]

8. Jefferson D. Ray, *Expository Preaching* (Grand Rapids: Zondervan, 1940), p. 71.
9. Blackwood, *Preaching from the Bible*, p. 39.
10. Ibid., p. 95.
11. Meyer, p. 32.

The systematic, book-by-book method of preaching has been my approach for over fifteen years. More and more its value becomes apparent. There is no better way to convey the truths of God's Word.

EXPOSITORY PREACHERS

There have been many great expository preachers. Alexander Maclaren was a fine expositor. He subjected himself to a very rigorous study schedule. Each day of the week he would shut himself away in his study. He did very little visiting and administrative work. To read his sermons is to read messages of unusual clarity and strength; his exegesis is extremely well done, his outlines are clear and to the point, his illustrations beautifully amplify the meaning of the passage, and he makes very good application to his hearers.

G. Campbell Morgan has been called the Prince of Expositors. In the beginning years of my own expository work G. Campbell Morgan's work was a good example for me. His ability to analyze a passage of Scripture taught me much. Morgan was a master of studying a passage in its total context. He could masterfully analyze a text, and with equal skill he could put the text back together in a beautiful logical sequence. Morgan would often read the book of the Bible he was going to preach from forty to fifty times during his preparation. He would take the book apart and then rebuild it with a simple, clear outline. In Morgan's opinion, determining an outline is the most important part of sermon preparation. The young preacher would be wise to read carefully Morgan's exposition of books of the Bible. Carefully study his approach. Though Morgan's content is excellent, his ability to analyze the passage will profit you the most.

Donald Grey Barnhouse, too, was a fine expository preacher. Perhaps his greatest work is his multivolume set on Romans, a masterpiece of paragraph-by-paragraph exposition through a book of the Bible. Barnhouse explained his method of exposition like this: He would take the whole Bible and bring it to bear on his particular preaching passage. To read Barnhouse's work on Romans is to virtually give oneself a thorough education in the entire Bible.

W. A. Criswell, beloved pastor of First Baptist Church, Dallas, Texas, has gained an international reputation as a Bible expositor. His books are veritable storehouses of information and guidance for the preacher who would preach expository messages. His volumes on Revelation are among the finest. His word study is excellent, and his interpretation is clear and concise. Though a clearly discernible outline does not often appear, the preacher will learn a great deal about expository preaching by a careful study of Criswell's work. Criswell was invaluable to me as I began my own expository preaching.

APPROACHES TO EXPOSITORY PREACHING

There are several different approaches to the expository method. One is the *running commentary*. Farris D. Whitesell, in his helpful volume on sermon preparation, does not believe this is expository preaching, but I believe it can properly fit the category. The running commentary method lacks a discernible outline; the primary focus of the message is upon the text itself rather than upon an outline. All the constituent elements of a sermon are included with the exception of an outline. A sermon is primarily expository because of the way the passage is handled. To that degree the running commentary may be classified as an expository sermon.

H. A. Ironside often used the running commentary. Ironside's commentaries on various books of the Bible have a simplicity of interpretation and clarity of application that are very fresh and helpful. Homer G. Lindsay, Jr., my partner in ministry, uses this particular method. From personal observation of Dr. Lindsay's preaching I know this method can be extremely effective. The messages are easily adaptable to the particular needs of the congregation.

There is one great danger in the running commentary. The preacher can depend upon his thoughts about the passage at the moment rather than give himself to rigorous study of the passage—The temptation is to give too little preparation to the message. Further, the absence of an outline weakens the sermon's structure. One's ability to retain the substance of the sermon is also lessened. But this method seems to work quite well for some men, and so it should not be casually dismissed.

Another approach is through *Bible reading*. This is somewhat different from the running commentary approach. The preacher reads a section, gives some explanation and application, then moves to the next section. This has the same advantages and disadvantages as the running commentary method.

Pure exposition of a passage with very little structure is another method. Here little attempt is made to give any balance or beauty to the scant outline. Very little work is done in providing subpoints under the main points. Probably most of the men who do expository work tend to fall in this category. Some men use this approach quite well. Those who have an obvious gift for teaching find pure exposition extremely adaptable to their purposes. There is much to commend it.

The finest type of expository preaching is the *expository sermonizing* method. This method reflects understanding of the passage on the part of the preacher. He prepares a logical presentation of the content of the message. He has a main topic, main divisions, an introduction, and a conclusion. Using this structure he will by means of illustration, argumentation, and explanation make the passage clear to the people and apply its truths to their lives. Let me encourage the young preacher to begin using this method.

The expository method of preaching exalts Jesus Christ. The great aim of our preaching is to make Christ known to our people. We do not want our people to leave church on Sunday declaring what great preachers we are; we want them to leave thrilled about what a wonderful Savior we have. The thrust and aim of all our preaching must be Jesus Christ. We must say with Paul, "For I determined not to know anything among you, save Jesus Christ, and Him crucified" (1 Cor. 2:2). Only the preaching of Christ brings men to God. Again Paul says, "It pleased God by the foolishness of preaching to save them that believe . . . but we preach Christ crucified" (1 Cor. 1:21, 23).

As we preach Christ using the expository method we will make a marvelous discovery. Many passages of Scripture, when first read, will seem rather obscure, perhaps even uninteresting, and hardly worth our attention. As we continue to read, however, suddenly the Lord Jesus Christ appears in the passage. Having found Him we discover a treasure chest of riches. On the Lord's day, as we preach Jesus from that passage, the whole congregation will be greatly enriched. I recommend to you the expository method with all the emphasis I can muster. As we continue to unfold this method you will share with me the excitement and the blessing of Bible exposition.

Biblical Roots of the Expository Method

The expository method of preaching has strong, deep roots in the Old and New Testaments. I am indebted to Dr. Paige Patterson for pointing me toward a very helpful terminology for preaching in both the Old and New Testaments (Paige Patterson, homiletics class notes, Criswell Center for Biblical Studies, Dallas).

OLD TESTAMENT TERMINOLOGY

I have always wondered why the eighth chapter of Nehemiah is so seldom used as an illustration of an effective Bible worship service. Virtually every ingredient of a worship service is present. Ezra, the scribe, stood upon a pulpit of wood with the book of the law of Moses in his hand. The people gathered themselves together in a spirit of unity and expectancy. Ezra proclaimed God's Word; the people responded with amens and prostrated themselves before the Lord in worship. What a magnificent worship passage! In verses 7 and 8 we are given the method the Levites used in teaching the people the law of God. Verse 8 says, "so they read in the book in the law of God distinctly, and gave the sense, and caused them to understand the reading."

Several terms from these verses help us understand Old Testament preaching. "Distinctly" is the Hebrew word *pārash*, which means to distinguish or to specify clearly.[12] The idea of clarity in making understanding possible is paramount. Further, the Levites "gave the sense." The Hebrew word is *śēkel*, which means to give the sense of the meaning; perception or insight is indicated.[13] Further, the verses say the Levites "caused them to understand the reading." The word for "caused them to understand" is *bîn*, which means to separate mentally or to assist in understanding. That is a very good picture of what expository preaching is all about.

Dr. Patterson has listed several other Old Testament words that help us understand preaching. He includes *nābî*, which conveys the idea of one who pours forth or announces. Included is the thought of

12. Benjamin Davis and Edward C. Mitchell, *Student's Hebrew Lexicon* (Grand Rapids: Zondervan, 1960), p. 524.
13. Ibid., p. 639.

being moved by divine impulse to prophesy.[14] The word is found in Deuteronomy 13:1; Deuteronomy 18:20; Jeremiah 23:21. Numbers 11:25-29 illustrates well the meaning of the word. In this passage we are told that the spirit that was upon Moses came upon the seventy elders. When the spirit rested upon them they prophesied. In verse 29 Moses declared, "Would God that all the Lord's people were prophets, and that the Lord would put his spirit upon them!" We see here that Old Testament preaching was of divine origin. The idea of pouring forth a message that came from God is given prominence.

Several times in the Old Testament the word *seer* is used. Two Hebrew words are translated thus. One of them, *hōzeh* (e.g., Amos 7:12), conveys the idea of to glow or to grow warm. The other word, *rōéh*, means one who sees. In 1 Chronicles 29:29 we are told Samuel was the seer. Isaiah 30:10 also makes reference to the seer. These terms suggest that the prophet was one whose heart had been warmed by something the Lord allowed him to see.

In Ecclesiastes 1:1 the word *qōhelet* is used, meaning a caller or preacher. Sometimes the word means a lecturer. The root word is *qāhal*, which means to assemble together.[15] Thus, a preacher is one who speaks before an assembly of people who have been gathered together.

Another word used for preaching in the Old Testament is *qārā'*, which means to call out. The word is found in Isaiah 61:1. The preacher calls to the people. He addresses the message of God to them. A similar word is *bāśar*, which means to be fresh or full, or to announce glad tidings. This is found in Isaiah 61:1 and Psalms 40:9. The preacher is one who brings good news.

NEW TESTAMENT TERMINOLOGY

In the New Testament many helpful pictures of preaching situations are given. Our Lord Jesus Himself was a preacher. Luke 24:27 indicates that He used the expository method. Verse 27 reads, "And beginning at Moses and all the prophets, He expounded unto them in all the scriptures the things concerning himself." The word translated "expounded" is the Greek word *diermēneuō,* which means "to unfold

14. Ibid., p. 392.
15. Ibid., p. 555.

the meaning of what is said," to explain through or "expound."

Two characteristics of expository preaching are seen in the method of our Lord. First, His method reveals a systematic presentation of Scripture. Beginning at Moses and in all the prophets He "explained through" the Scriptures. That certainly suggests the idea of consecutive preaching. What a marvelous exposition those two disciples must have heard as Jesus began at Genesis and moved consecutively through the Old Testament! The expository preacher has the same wonderful privilege.

Further, we observe that Jesus gave a Christ-centered presentation of Scripture. We are told that Jesus expounded in all the Scriptures the things concerning Himself. All genuine exposition culminates in Jesus. Spurgeon said that he took a text and beat a path to Jesus; if there was no path, he said, he made one. True New Testament preaching must exalt the Lord Jesus. Some sermons I have heard would have been just as appropriate in a Jewish synagogue. No preaching can be called New Testament if the Lord Jesus Christ is not magnified.

The apostle Paul was one of the greatest New Testament preachers. His preaching method is set before us in Acts 17:2-3. These verses show the phenomenal ministry Paul had in Thessalonica. Paul probably stayed there less than one month, yet his letters to believers in that place give evidence of a growing, solid congregation. What kind of preaching did Paul do? Three words give us our answer. We are told that for three Sabbath days he "reasoned with them out of the scriptures, opening and alleging, that Christ must needs have suffered, and risen again from the dead."

The word "reasoned" is *dialegomai,* "to speak through." The idea of pondering or revolving in the mind is intended. The word came to mean to converse with or to discuss. Bible exposition is a logical presentation of Scripture. Effective exposition must be clear and understandable. This particular word also suggests that good exposition builds around a theme and draws its main points from the Scripture verses themselves.

The word "opening" is *dianoigō,* which means to open thoroughly. Thayer explains the word means to open the sense of the Scriptures or to explain them.[16] Paul opened up the meaning of Scripture to the people. The same word is used in Luke 24:32, "Did not

16. Joseph Henry Thayer, *Greek-English Lexicon* (Grand Rapids: Zondervan, 1963).

our heart burn within us, while he talked with us by the way, and while he opened to us the scriptures?" Jesus also opened up the Scriptures when He preached. Expository preaching is an explanatory presentation of the Scriptures. The Bible method is to draw from the passage itself the substance of the sermon.

The word "alleging" is used to describe Paul's preaching method. The Greek word is *parathithēmi,* which means to place alongside. This indicates that Paul's preaching was an applicable presentation of Scripture. The word is used in Matthew 13:34, where we are told, "All these things spake Jesus unto the multitude in parables." Jesus took parables, laid them alongside the issues of life faced by the people to whom He spoke, and made practical application. The faithful Bible preacher takes the meaning of the word of God and places it alongside the daily lives of those who listen to him. Thus he makes personal, specific application to the hearers.

In addition to those particular terms, Dr. Patterson has listed other New Testament terminology. The word *logos* is used to refer to a word or saying. Sometimes the communication of God's message to man is referred to as preaching the Word (*Logos*). Another word, *rhēma,* emphasizes that which has been uttered by the living voice. The word is so used in Romans 10:17, indicating that God communicates Himself in the act of preaching. Therefore, preaching is in actuality divine instruction by those who communicate the gospel (see Eph. 3:17). First Peter 1:25 says, "But the word of the Lord endureth forever." In this passage the word *rhema* is used. The preacher delivers a message that has inherent life because God communicates Himself in His truth. The preacher has the glorious privilege of communicating the very life of God through His life-giving Word.

The frequently used word *kērussō* means to proclaim after the manner of a herald. The idea is a message of authority that calls upon the listeners to read and to obey. Romans 10:14-15 uses this term. Also, the word is found in 1 Corinthians 1:21, 23, and 2 Timothy 4:2. The New Testament preacher was one who proclaimed the message of the King of kings to men. There is an atmosphere of seriousness and authority implied in the word. The preacher does not proclaim a message derived from his own heart; his preaching has an authority given him by God.

Another frequently used word is *evangelizō,* meaning to announce glad tidings, or to bring good news. Specifically, it refers to the good news of salvation that God gives to men in Christ Jesus. In Luke 4:18, Christ's ministry was to announce the good news. The New Testament preachers went everywhere announcing the good news (see Acts 8:4). When Philip gave the gospel to the Ethiopian eunuch, we are told in Acts 8:35, "Then Philip opened his mouth, and began at the same scripture, and preached unto him Jesus." The preacher of the Bible announces God's good news from heaven. There is a note of joy and victory in the word. There are places where the emphasis of *evangelizō* seems to be upon the privilege of every believer to announce the salvation that is in Christ Jesus. That emphasis has its proper place in the ministry of a faithful Bible preacher, and true Bible preaching must always be evangelistic in nature.

Sometimes preaching is referred to as a message of encouragement. The Greek word *parakaleō* means "to call to one's side." It carries the idea of comfort, exhortation, and instruction. The ideas of strength and encouragement are embedded in the word. Paul admonishes the young preacher Timothy to "Exhort with all longsuffering and doctrine" (2 Tim. 4:2). Romans 12:8 says that exhortation is a spiritual gift. The man who has been called to preach the Bible will be gifted by the Holy Spirit to bring strength and encouragement to those who listen to him preach. This aspect of preaching is greatly needed in every age, and especially this one. Every Bible preacher needs to read the command of Hebrews 3:13, "But exhort one another daily, while it is called To day."

Sometimes preaching is viewed as giving a witness. The word *martureō* is sometimes used to explain what preaching is. The word means simply to be a witness or to affirm that one has seen, heard, or experienced something. Paul, in his beautiful and insightful summary of his ministry at Ephesus, gives a simple definition of his preaching. He defines his preaching content as "testifying . . . repentance toward God, and faith toward our Lord Jesus Christ" (Acts 20:21). The preacher who faithfully proclaims the truth of the Bible must not do so from secondhand experience. His message must be real to him. The preacher must know to be true what he preaches to others. The Bible preacher must be able to say in the words of 1 John 4:14, "We have seen and do testify that the Father sent the Son to be the Saviour of the world."

Another word used to describe New Testament preaching is *hom-ologeō*. This word, made of two Greek words, means "to say the same thing" or "to agree with." Preaching in the New Testament sense has the idea of confession or profession. In 1 Timothy 6:12 Paul says about young Timothy that he has "professed a good profession before many witnesses." Rightly understood, Bible preaching is confessional in nature. The preacher says what God says. He agrees with God about the truth he proclaims.

New Testament preaching also includes the element of rebuke or conviction. The word *elegchō* is sometimes used in relationship to preaching. The thought conveyed is by conviction to bring to light, or to expose. Titus 1:9 says that we "may be able by sound doctrine both to exhort and to convince the gainsayers." Titus 2:15 commands the preacher, "Rebuke with all authority." There are times when the faithful expositor of the Word must deal directly with the sins of the people. By preaching the Word he turns on the light so that his hearers may see themselves as God sees them. This kind of preaching, done with compassion and courage, should bring the listener to a point of conviction so that he will turn from his sin and to God for cleansing.

New Testament preaching also includes the element of teaching. Jesus was a teacher. New Testament preachers were teachers. We are commissioned to teach. The word is *didaskō*. Acts 5:42 says the apostles "ceased not to teach and preach Jesus Christ." In listing the requirements of the bishop-pastor 1 Timothy 3:2 says, "A bishop then must be . . . apt to teach." The importance of teaching Bible doctrine cannot be overestimated. Preachers must teach their people basic Bible doctrine. That can be most effectively done by using the expository method of sermon preparation. Second Timothy 2:2 urges, "The same commit thou to faithful men, who shall be able to teach others also."

Second Peter 1:20 uses an interesting word. The word is *epiluō*, which means literally "to unloose" or "to untie."[17] The word conveys the idea of explaining what is obscure and hard to understand. Thus, the word means to interpret. This word is used in Mark 4:34, where we are told of the preaching ministry of Jesus and His use of the parable: "When they were alone, he [Jesus] expounded all things to his disciples." Preaching is unloosing a passage of Scripture. The passage is untied so that the accurate meaning can be understood.

17. Ibid., p. 240.

That is a beautiful insight into the expository method: the expository preacher takes a passage of Scripture and "unties it" for the people. After the message is over the people should have a better understanding of that particular passage.

In Acts 20:11 Paul was preaching in Troas. The Scripture says he "talked a long while, even till break of day." The verb used is *homileō*, which means "to converse," or "talk with." It has the idea of engaging in conversation.[18] The Bible preacher is not merely giving a soliloquy. The preacher preaches; the people listen; there is feedback between them. *Homileō* is used in Luke 24:14 to describe the conversation the two disciples on the Emmaus road had concerning the events of the Lord's crucifixion in Jerusalem.

Another word used of New Testament preaching is *peithō*, meaning to "persuade others with words" to believe. We find the word so used in describing the preaching of Paul in Acts 18:4: "And he reasoned in the synagogue every Sabbath, and persuaded the Jews and the Greeks." The Bible preacher is a persuader. By use of Bible preaching he brings men to the point of believing Jesus is the Christ and deciding to commit themselves to the Lord. The effective expository preacher will learn how to utilize every possible method of persuasion.

Another word used in relationship to Bible preaching in the New Testament is *suzēteō*, meaning "to seek," or "to examine together." In Acts 9:29 we are told of Paul, "And he spoke boldly in the name of the Lord Jesus, and disputed against the Grecians." The New Testament preacher seeks to lead his listeners to examine with him the truths of God's Word and to seek an understanding of them.

Sometimes the word *apologia* is used. This word suggests a verbal defense or a speech in defense of. In 1 Peter 3:15 we are urged, "Be ready always to give an answer to every man." In Acts 22:1 Paul says, "Men, brethren, and fathers, hear ye my defense which I make now unto you." The Bible preacher, in the best sense of the term, is giving a defense for the gospel. Other passages use the same terminology (see Phil. 1:7 and 17; 2 Tim. 4:16). Bible preachers present the message of the Lord Jesus in the most convincing, appealing way possible.

In summarizing the Bible terms for preaching, several charac-

18. Ibid., p. 444.

teristics of preaching emerge. There is a solemnity and seriousness to preaching because God Himself is communicated therein. The substance of preaching is the Word of God. Preaching centers on Jesus Christ and is proclaimed enthusiastically. There is active interplay between preacher and congregation. The preacher must be divinely commissioned and gifted for this sacred task.

Good Bible preaching has several distinguishing characteristics. There is faithful proclamation of the good news. The people receive encouragement and instruction. It is done with all the persuasiveness the preacher can muster. The preacher preaches from the viewpoint of personal witnessing. He preaches what he knows in his own experience to be true.

We are on solid biblical ground when we adopt the expository method. The expository preacher is in the noble line of Nehemiah, Moses, the prophets, Paul and the apostles, and the Lord Jesus Christ Himself. The preacher who determines in his heart to follow the expository method can have confidence that God will bless him.

Advantages of the Expository Method

It is obvious that I am very much disposed toward the expository method of sermon preparation. A careful consideration of the advantages perhaps will convince you to give the method a good, earnest attempt. But in fairness I want to also give some consideration to a number of disadvantages that have been suggested.

SUPPOSED DISADVANTAGES

"Expository preaching is dull." It is said that expository preaching is always the same old thing. There is no up-to-date application of truth to people where they live. In all honesty I must say this is true of many expository sermons I have heard. This is not the fault of the method. Rather, the problem is in the faulty preparation and delivery of the preacher himself.

Expository preaching need not be dull. Expository sermons can be extremely interesting and positively relevant to the listeners. What use is a sermon if it does not relate to the listeners in a practical manner? We are not preaching merely to expose our people to information. The Bible is truth that transforms lives. There is absolutely no need for the expository preacher to be dull.

Sometimes the expository sermon is dull because of the sameness of approach: the preacher becomes pedantic; every message has the same kind of introduction; each message has points that are predictable; and the conclusion never has an original thought. That can bore the people out of their minds. But it need not be so. One of my purposes is to help you avoid those difficulties.

"Preaching through books of the Bible in an expository fashion does not allow for the leading of the Holy Spirit in sermon preparation." It seems to me such criticism is defective. Is the Holy Spirit limited in His guidance to one week at a time? Cannot the Holy Spirit lead us to preach through a book of the Bible as well as lead us to a text week after week? Let us not limit the Holy Spirit in this manner. Without question the Spirit of God has given me clear direction to preach certain books of the Bible to my congregation. The amazing appropriateness of the messages week by week has demonstrated that this is true. Many times as I have progressed through a book of the Bible I have been thrilled to see the Holy Spirit apply particular passages to specific problems in the lives of my people week after week!

Let me hasten to say that preaching through books of the Bible need not restrict you for weeks on end. If the preacher senses the leading of the Holy Spirit to preach on a particular text, let him by all means do so. He can always detour and preach the text God's Spirit impresses upon him. But he has a "home base" to come back to. Often in the midst of a book series I have been led to deliver one or two or even more messages to my people. After finishing those messages I have gone back to my book series and completed it. The expository method does not limit the leadership of the Holy Spirit.

"Expository messages have poor sermonic structure." I can understand this criticism, for very often the expository approach is subjected to poor sermonic presentation. But as I have said, expository preaching at its very best is built around a central theme and has well-organized points deriving from the message. The expository message must have good illustration, argumentation, and application. This criticism again is directed at poor *use* of exposition.

"Expository sermons degenerate into merely reading verses and making comments." This is often true. The preacher who gets into

this kind of trap will face the temptation to do very little preparation. Expository preaching is not adequately done unless the preacher prepares in the most comprehensive way possible. This also is a criticism of exposition at its worst, not at its best.

ADVANTAGES TO THE PREACHER

Using the expository method makes it possible for the preacher to learn the Word. By a careful, exegetical study through books of the Bible in preparation for sermons the preacher can come to master his Bible. One of the reasons for the great lack of Bible education on the part of Christian people is the "hop, skip, and jump" approach to Bible study. The preacher who jumps from book to book and text to text in his preaching ministry will greatly impoverish his own understanding of the Word. Such an approach is very similar to the "lucky dip" method. I remember a dear old saint in one of my country pastorates who used this approach to do her daily Bible reading. She would close her eyes, let her Bible fall open, and read at that particular opening. Who can question that she indeed received some value from her method? But she could have profited from her Bible much more by a systematic, book-by-book reading. The same holds true for the preacher.

Preaching expository messages through books of the Bible keeps the preacher out of a rut. Preachers have a tendency to develop a one-subject mentality. Preaching through different books of the Bible avoids that temptation. Every preacher has his special interests and gifts: some are drawn to the second coming passages of Scripture; others love those that make strong ethical applications; still others like the deeper life sections. The expository method keeps the preacher off his hobbyhorse. The Bible is like a magnificent fruit grove with all kinds of trees. Some love apples best, but there are also pears and cherries and bananas to be enjoyed.

The expository method guards against using the Bible as a club. Who among us has not felt, and even yielded to, the temptation to find a Scripture to rebuke an errant member? Clearly that is not a proper approach to the preaching of God's Word. Taking a book of the Bible and preaching its truths consecutively avoids that problem.

The expository method allows the Word of God—rather than our own inclinations—to speak to the current situation. Many years ago, as I was preaching through the book of James, I came to James's section on the tongue in chapter 3. After the service that morning one of my deacons rushed up to me and exclaimed, "Preacher, how did you know, how did you know?"

I replied, "How did I know what?"

"How did you know Mrs. Smith (not her real name) was going to be here this morning?"

In amazement I answered, "I don't know Mrs. Smith. What do you mean?" Mrs. Smith was the town gossip. She was famous for her biting, sarcastic tongue. She had never been to our church before. On the first time (and I am sure, the last time) she attended our church I spoke on the tongue. It was not accidental. As we faithfully proclaim the Word of God, the Holy Spirit will apply the truths of the Word to our listeners.

Expository preaching enables us to deal with passages that might otherwise have been overlooked or even intentionally avoided. There are sometimes delicate subjects dealt with in the Bible, and the temptation is to dodge them. But when we meet them in an expository series, we must deal with them at that point. Book-by-book exposition enables us to do so without creating the impression we are "picking on" some member of the church. For instance, should you come to the subject of divorce in the course of expository preaching, the people will not be curious to know why you chose that particular text for that Sunday. But if out of the clear blue sky you preach on divorce, the people will probably wonder why.

The expository method makes the preacher work. This is one of its greatest advantages. The preacher should not work less than his people. A lazy preacher is inexcusable. You cannot be lazy and do the necessary preparation to develop and deliver an expository sermon. You will be up early and study long. That is good, because preaching is not effective unless it comes through agony and suffering on the part of the preacher. To stand in the pulpit unprepared, with little forethought, and deliver a message off the top of your head is not worthy of the Savior you represent.

Preaching through books of the Bible removes anxiety about what to preach. In the earlier years of my ministry when I was preaching on topics, the weekly search for a text was a real agony to me. I have always been studious by nature; to me, the call to preach was a call to study. Many times I spent the whole week searching, scratching, studying to find a text. I would come to Saturday with no clear sense of direction. Many a preacher frantically searches through sermon books by some well-known preacher to find a message for Sunday. The expository method relieves this formidable problem. On Monday morning you know where you are going. You can begin your preparation immediately. During the week, should the Lord lead you to preach on another subject, fine; the next Monday you will be just that much ahead. Believe me, brethren, this is the way to go. Would it not be much better to have the entire week to study a passage rather than spending most of the week searching for one?

Expository preaching gives great confidence to the preacher. When he stands to preach, he is aware he has given himself to serious and sincere study of the Word. He stands behind the sacred desk with a sense that he speaks from the authority of the Bible, not his own. He is merely the mouth and lips through which the living Word of God is conveyed to the congregation. He is confident that he is not speaking merely his own thoughts or opinions. He is speaking "thus saith the Lord." That gives immense force to a ministry.

ADVANTAGES TO THE PEOPLE

There are also numerous advantages to the people who listen to expository sermons.

Expository preaching gives people strength. There is a great heart-hunger on the part of people for the Word of God. Never have I seen an appetite for the Word as I am witnessing at the present time. The expository sermon preaches to that heart-hunger. Charles W. Koller mentions that nutritionists use the term "nutritional timebomb" with reference to certain deficiencies in one's diet that may remain undetected for years. Those deficiencies can suddenly manifest themselves in severe sickness. The same is true for those who are undernourished in their spiritual lives. Without a proper diet of Bible preaching and teaching, the stress of sudden catastrophe or unusual burden make the spiritually undernourished too weak to weather the storm.[19]

19. Charles W. Koller, *Expository Preaching Without Notes* (Grand Rapids: Baker, 1962), pp. 29-34.

That need not happen to God's people. As the pastor faithfully preaches the Word of God, the people receive strength. There is built within them a reservoir of Bible truth that will enable them to face times of crisis. As a pastor I have witnessed through many years that God's people come through with great victory and triumph if they have been fed a solid Bible diet. I have been amazed and blessed at the strength God's people have displayed in emergency situations.

The lack of moral strength and convictions that plagues our day is due, to a large degree, to the lack of Bible preaching in the pulpits in recent years. A return to the strong, systematic preaching of Bible truths can do much to reverse the tide of immorality that threatens to engulf us. As the believer understands the moral implications of his faith he gains the adequate materials with which to build a genuinely moral life.

Expository preaching encourages the people to become students of the Word themselves. Through the years I have seen expository preaching through books of the Bible give the people an appetite for the Word. It has sent the people home to search the Scriptures for themselves. They become "Berean" Christians. In Acts 17:11, we are told that the believers of Berea "were more noble than those in Thessalonica, in that they received the Word with all readiness of mind, and searched the scriptures daily, whether those things were so." I have been amazed at the Bible knowledge many of God's people have acquired as result of the expository method of preaching.

I have also seen people with limited education become fine Bible teachers. This is perhaps the best way to train people in the church to become Bible teachers. As the pastor teaches the Word of God he also shows his people how to teach the Word to others. Many fine Sunday school teachers can be developed in this way.

I have been blessed in my own ministry to see many young men answer the call to preach, and many times I have wondered why. I believe one reason is the emphasis I have placed upon expository sermon preparation and delivery. As those young men have listened to and observed my preaching, they have been challenged to minister the Word to others. Of course, I recognize there has to be a divine call to preach—but there is surely something to be said about the importance of role models for the young men in our churches.

Expository preaching has a way of broadening people's horizons.

Expository sermons enable them to glimpse the eternal. Bible truths such as justification, glorification, eternity, and the Spirit-filled life lift people to new heights of Bible knowledge and Christian experience. They are given the opportunity to see a world of Christian existence that they never dreamed possible. If my own life is enriched through expository preaching, I can be confident my people's lives will be enriched as well.

Expository preaching will provide the preacher with an increasingly maturing congregation. I have made a careful study of successful pastorates, and in almost every instance, the church has been blessed by the ministry of a pastor who spent many years with the same congregation. Most of those pastors have also been strong expositors of the Word. They have actually "preached through" their problems. Many a pastor started with a very immature congregation, began preaching through books of the Bible, and so helped foster spirituality. As both pastor and people mature in the Lord, they are able to do the work of the Lord together in a more harmonious and effective fashion. Bible preaching makes for a strong and healthy church congregation.

The preacher must be with his people if he is to know their problems; he must fellowship with God if he is to have solutions to those problems. The expository method of preaching will help bring about those two positive benefits. As the preacher studies to preach through books of the Bible, his own soul will be healthy and mature. As he preaches the messages to the people, they will grow and mature as well. The result will be a very happy combination.

SOME DANGERS

The advantages of the expository method far outweigh any disadvantage that might be imagined. But there are some dangers to be avoided.

The expository preacher must be very careful not to become monotonous in his exposition. Sometimes, because of the similarity of content throughout a particular book of the Bible, the preacher may fall into a sameness in his introduction, the way he states his points, and in his general approach to the message. This can be avoided. The great expositors have been able to sustain the interest of people through a lengthy series of expositions. Donald Grey Barnhouse preached three and one-half years from the book of Romans in the morning services, and his congregation grew continually through those years until the building was filled. W. A. Criswell took eighteen years to preach through the entire Bible; his First Baptist Church in Dallas grew phenomenally during those years.

We know that some men are more gifted than others in holding the attention of the people. The knowledge of certain aspects of delivery can make the sermon more interesting and exciting. At all times let the preacher be looking for variety in exposition. There may be times when he will want to preach from a shorter passage. Why not bring a message from a single verse? Donald Grey Barnhouse did that very effectively in his series through the book of Romans. Again, expository preaching depends not so much on the length of the passage as in the manner of its treatment. Take a single verse in your book exposition and preach that verse. Draw your theme and main points from that verse. Give it a new twist. Or, when you come to a very important doctrinal word in a paragraph, why not bring a message on that great doctrine in an expository fashion?

Here is another method I have used that has helped avoid monotony in expository preaching: Sometimes between my book studies I have inserted a brief series on another subject. Using ten to twelve messages I have preached a series on subjects such as: great events in the life of Christ; great interviews in the life of Jesus; and the miracles of Jesus. All of those messages were developed in an expository fashion. But some variety was given from week-by-week exposition of a book of the Bible.

The expository preacher can go into too much detail. He can try to examine every minute part of every verse in a passage. This was evidently the approach of many Puritan divines. The Puritans preached many, many years on a single book, which probably accounts for their very small congregations.[20] The preacher should study every minute detail of his preaching passage. He should carefully go over the details of the grammar. He should look carefully at the tenses of the verb. He should be very aware of the different prepositions in the passage, and may even give attention to the definite articles. But that does not mean he should bring all of that technical baggage into the

20. George Henderson, *Lectures to Young Preachers* (Edinburgh: B. McCall Barbour, 1961), p. 88.

pulpit. Give the people the cream of your study; don't beat them to death with excessive material. You would probably be shocked to learn how little of your message the people retain anyway. Drive for the main lessons of the passage. Give them the big picture. Don't weary them with the small, insignificant details.

Just a few months ago I heard one of our finest contemporary expositors. He was bringing a series on one aspect of the Christmas message. It was obvious he had researched the subject thoroughly. I learned more about those certain Christmas characters than I had ever learned in all my life; I do not question a multivolume study could be presented on the basis of that expositor's research. But after listening for several days to his presentation, my response was: So what? In spite of my admiration and respect for this great expositor, I found myself actually bored. His minute study of details had caused me to completely lose interest.

No method of Bible preaching is without its dangers. But the benefits of the expository method are quite worth every danger the preacher may risk. In this book I hope to give you approaches and methods that will enable you to avoid those dangers. Again let me urge you to become an expositor of the Word. If you will give yourself to Bible exposition, you will find you are in a field where you have no competitors. Try to discuss politics with your people—someone else will be more knowledgeable. Become an expert in the social questions of the day—you will discover your knowledge is too limited. Become a philosopher—and find yourself speaking to an empty building. Become a Bible expositor and you will be pleased to discover that people from all walks of life will come to hear you.

A few years ago a fine young professor moved to our city to head the chemistry department of a local college. He and his family visited our church. The next week I visited in his home. Almost immediately he said to me: "Preacher, I deal with chemistry and mathematics all during the week. When I come to church on Sunday I want to know what God says in the Bible." I have never forgotten those words. In your congregation may be doctors who are skilled in medicine, teachers who are experts in their field, and businessmen who are geniuses in finance. But chances are most of them are in kindergarten biblically and spiritually. They want to hear from a man who has been with God in His Word during the week. They want to hear a preacher who can proclaim from the Word the realities of life and the answers for the deepest needs of their hearts.

That is the reason for our attempt to help you in sermon preparation. I want you to become "a workman that needeth not to be ashamed, rightly dividing the word of truth" (2 Tim. 2:15).

2

The Preparation of Pastor and People

Preparation is an important element in good expository preaching. The preacher must not only spend time preparing the message; he must also prepare himself. God's Word is not preached apart from human instrumentality—what the preacher is and what he believes hold a vital place in good sermon preparation.

Seven sections are included in this chapter. First is a discussion of the integrity of the expository preacher, including a brief survey of biblical standards for the preacher. This will give you an opportunity to carefully evaluate your own life in light of the standards set forth in the New Testament.

The second section, on convictions about the Word of God, should be carefully studied. What the preacher believes about the Bible will be determinative in his preaching ministry. Some space is given to discussing the authority of the Scriptures and one's personal convictions about that authority. I want to encourage you to take a high view of the inspiration of Scripture.

I consider the devotional life of the preacher to be the real key to effectiveness in expository preaching. Much of the third section is personal in nature—sharing with you my own devotional life. I do not do so as the final authority, but as one giving suggestions that may assist you in developing a strong devotional life of your own.

The preacher must maintain a definite program of continuing intellectual development; formal training is important. The pastor who is the role model for the younger preacher is a definite part of that training. In the fourth section I emphasize the need to maintain a lifetime of continuing intellectual development. Fifth, I will give some practical suggestions about the location of the study, time of study, and tools of study. Sixth, there is a brief section on physical fitness; the chapter closes with a section on how to prepare your people for the expository preaching ministry.

Give attention to making yourself the man of God you ought to be. Making yourself a better messenger will assist you in preparing better messages.

The Integrity of the Expositor

You may find this chapter a little "preachy"; that is what I intend! Preaching the Bible is an altogether unique enterprise, for God's Word cannot be preached effectively when there is something awry in the personal life. God wants His vessels to be clean. One may teach algebra adequately and not pay one's bills, but no one can adequately expound the Word of God and fail to pay his bills. One can be sexually immoral and serve as a grocery clerk, but no one can preach the Word of God in that condition. A man's personal life and discipline can make or break his preaching ministry.

Before I begin a discussion of the mechanics of the expository method I must challenge you to a point of decision. This is not merely opinion on my part. The Bible makes very clear that the preacher preaches by his life as well as by his lips: there is a sense in which what a man *is* is more important than what he says. There is great strength in the silent sermon of a godly life. As we shall see in the three examples below, all through the Scriptures the importance of personal, practical godliness is emphasized.

FIRST THESSALONIANS 2:1-12

In this intimate and intensely personal passage the apostle Paul sets forth his own convictions about the secrets of genuine pastoral leadership. Paul seems to open up his heart and allow us to enter. Just what does Paul set forth as the ideal for an effective pastor? As a reading of the chapter reveals, the qualifications are far different from what is ordinarily thought.

Today's image of the successful pastor and effective preacher is of a man who is unusually handsome. He has the voice of an actor and the mind of a scholar. Not so, according to Paul. In the first two verses Paul indicates he felt a strong sense of mission. His previous trials and tribulations in Philippi were enough to send weaker men scurrying for home. Why did Paul not give up the mission? The reason is obvious. He felt a commitment to the gospel of God that made him bold under the most difficult of circumstances. The work of preaching is no easy task. There is no easy way to do it. When you set out on a mission to serve the Lord you can be sure you will encounter many difficult obstacles along the way. Only a sense of mission such as Paul expresses can keep you going under such circumstances.

In verses 3-6 Paul discusses his own preaching ministry, and so gives us helpful guidelines in the matter of personal integrity. When he refers to "our exhortation" he is not simply talking about a particular message, nor about his delivery. He is going to the depths of his own motives. In Paul's time there were false teachers who moved from place to place preying on the people. Sadly, we face the same problem today: charlatans on television and radio have caused large numbers of people to be skeptical of preachers in general. Because of that, our motives must be right.

Paul answers a threefold charge that was apparently leveled against his own motives. He emphatically states that his preaching was "not of deceit, nor of uncleanness, nor in guile" (v. 3). He is saying that his message is true, his motives are pure, and his methods are above question. He is not attempting to please men, he is not using flattering words (v. 5). Someone has said that flattery is soft-soaping a person until he can't see for the suds. There is too much flattery in modern preaching. There is, of course, a right place for praise and compliment. But if we are to be pure in our motives, we must never flatter those to whom we preach for the sake of personal gain or praise. We must search our hearts to the depths. We must carefully ask ourselves at all times, Is my preaching genuinely motivated?

In verses 7-12 Paul discusses his manner among the people. These verses are a manual of instructions for the preacher who would effectively minister. Paul conducted himself in the midst of the people in a "gentle" manner. He obviously had a compassionate heart. His love for people is clearly revealed in the way he describes his manner among them. The true preacher will assume a threefold role, as did Paul.

Paul was to the people like a mother (v. 7-8). The picture here is actually of a mother in the nursery with her children. Picture a mother-nurse cherishing her little ones. Watch her as she caresses, feeds, hugs her babies. That is the manner of the true preacher. The mother will gladly give her life for the child. In verse 8 Paul says he would gladly have given his own soul for the people. When I was a boy I often heard the older preachers say at the conclusion of their messages, "Beloved, I have delivered my soul to you today." I did not really understand what they meant at the time. After many years of preaching, I understand. Real preaching is not only the delivery of a message; a life is also delivered. Preaching is not the performance of an hour; preaching is the outflow of a life.

Paul also teaches us to assume the role of a laborer. In verses 9-10 he indicates that his ministry was not confined to a forty-hour week. He poured his life into his labors. The preacher with integrity knows no office hours and punches no time clock. I am not saying the preacher does not need time with his family, time for recreation and other vital activities; but personal integrity demands that the man who preaches expository sermons to his people must be a hard worker. No member of your congregation should work harder at his job than you do at yours. How can a preacher in good conscience accept a salary from people who come to hear him preach if he spends little time in sermon preparation?

Finally Paul compares the preacher to a spiritual father (v. 11-12). There must be the tenderness of the mother in the preacher but also the firmness of the father. Personal integrity demands that the expository preacher be truthful with his people. He must speak lovingly, but firmly. Among other things, a father teaches the child how to walk. God's people are children in a royal family. We have a responsibility to teach them how to live the Christian life. That is a sacred responsibility. The very highest level of personal integrity is demanded.

FIRST TIMOTHY 3:1-7

Several passages in the New Testament set forth the personal character requirements of the preacher. Paul says in 1 Timothy 4:16, "Take heed unto thyself, and unto the doctrine"; Paul admonishes the young preacher Timothy to give attention first to his own character, then to the teaching. In the same book in chapter 3 Paul gives some of the personal requirements of the preacher. These may be familiar to you, but we need to constantly remind ourselves of them and use them as spiritual checkpoints.

First, we must be *blameless* (1 Tim. 3:2). That does not mean sinlessness; *blameless* carries the idea of being without reproach. There should be nothing in a preacher's conduct that would give anyone a reason to point a finger of rebuke toward his ministry. The preacher must be above reproach in his marriage relationship. The effectiveness of many a preacher is jettisoned by inconsistencies in his relationship to his wife.

Further, the preacher is to be *vigilant*. First Peter 5:8 explains this for us: "Be vigilant; because your adversary the devil, as a roaring lion, walketh about." The preacher must be always wary of subtle attempts on Satan's part to sabotage his ministry.

The word *sober* does not mean the preacher is not to get drunk, although that is certainly true. Rather the idea of being a man of calm, unimpassioned mind is intended. The preacher must be master of himself and his situation. He must also be *of good behavior*. He must not only talk well, but walk well. He must be *given to hospitality*. There is a surprising emphasis on this duty of preachers in the New Testament. We have the privilege to open our houses as well as our hearts to our people. He must also be *apt to teach*. The preacher guides the people through careful, consistent teaching of the Scriptures.

Further, Paul says the preacher is not to be *given to wine*. The word implies not sitting over the wine. He must be very careful about his personal habits. How can a preacher be effective in the pulpit when there is no discipline in his personal life? *No striker* means he must not be a violent man. He must avoid the combative spirit. He must also be *not greedy of filthy lucre*. The personal integrity of many a preacher has been wrecked by an undue attachment to money. Too many preachers get interested in some little "deal on the side." Valuable time that could be spent in sermon preparation is sometimes used for personal gain.

The preacher must also be *patient*. "Forbearing" is a better word. There must be that quality of heart that makes allowances for the inconsistencies and rudenesses of others. Next, he is *not* to be *a brawler*; he is to be a peaceable person. Let him not stir up strife in his daily dealings with people. Next, Paul urges, *not covetous*. The word Paul uses here actually means money-loving. The preacher is not to covet any possession or any place not his own.

In verse 4 Paul says the preacher must be *one that ruleth well his own house, having his children in subjection with all gravity*. What the preacher is and does with his own children will greatly help him in dealing with the children of God placed in his care. Further, he is *not* to be *a novice*. This means the preacher must have had opportunity to demonstrate in his life the kind of character that is projected in the gospel he preaches. He must also *have a good report*. The lost world very often is a shrewd judge of character. The preacher must not necessarily earn the approval of the world; instead, the world must have nothing it can truthfully use to discredit the preacher's ministry.

TITUS 1:5-9

A similar set of character requirements is found in Titus 1:5-9. Writing to another young preacher, Titus, Paul adds to his statements concerning the personal integrity of the preacher. In discussing the preacher's family, Paul says he should have *faithful children*. This could be rendered "believing children." The indication here is that the preacher will win his own children to the Lord. That may be the acid test for the preacher's integrity. Can the preacher lead his own children to put their trust in the Savior he proclaims in the pulpit? If the preacher lives his message before his children, they will be prone to follow him in a commitment to Jesus Christ.

In addition, Paul adds in verse 7 that the preacher is *not* to be *self-willed*. This means being overbearing or arrogant. The self-willed person is the one who never thinks of the desires of others; his way is the only way. He is the person who is so pleased with himself that nobody else pleases him, and he cares to please nobody. In addition, Paul says the preacher is *not* to be *soon angry*. This means not quick-tempered. The preacher must look closely at the deepest emotions of his life. I have met too many preachers who are angry men. It is sad they take their anger to the pulpit with them and spew it at the people.

Paul also adds in verse 8 that the preacher is to be *a lover of good men*. He is to be a supporter of the good. The preacher must be a good man who has a good heart and who surrounds himself with good things. Further, Paul adds the word *just*—he endeavors to be right with men. Next Paul says *holy*—the preacher should seek to be right with men and with God. Finally, Paul says the preacher is to be *temperate*. This conveys the idea of being inwardly strong. Temperance is the inner strength that enables the preacher to control his bodily appetites and passions.

There is only one way these divine standards for the preacher can be accomplished. No man is strong enough in himself to achieve such a rigorous standard of personal integrity. Only as God's men allow themselves to be controlled by the Holy Spirit can they be the kind of men who are pleasing to God and who are effective in ministering His Word.

Do not lightly consider these matters. They are absolutely essential. If you are not working hard to prepare yourself to be a better man, you are wasting your time learning how to prepare a better sermon.

Convictions Concerning the Word of God

There are those who believe one's view of the inspiration of Scripture is unimportant and not a factor in the matter of preaching. Andrew Blackwood in his book *Preaching from the Bible* says, "Fortunately a man's effectiveness in the pulpit does not depend upon his theory of inspiration."[1] I could not disagree more. I believe the preacher's view of inspiration is crucial in the matters of both sermon preparation and pulpit effectiveness.

There is no question in my mind that the reason for a sharp

1. Andrew Blackwood, *Preaching from the Bible* (New York: Abingdon, 1941), p. 182.

decline in preaching in this century is to be found right here. For many years in theological circles there has been widespread rejection of the doctrine of verbal plenary inspiration of the Word of God. The critics have insisted that the Bible is subject to errancy and human limitation. That has inevitably resulted in a sharp decline in Bible preaching. If the preacher loses his conviction that the Bible is the source of authority, why will he bother to preach from the Scriptures? Merrill F. Unger's statement is pertinent: "If the Bible is considered merely to contain the Word of God, rather than actually to be *in toto* the Word of God, there is naturally a decreased sense of responsibility to study its text minutely, or to systematize its theology, or authoritatively to declare its message."[2]

The Crisis of Authority

One's convictions concerning the Word of God will definitely affect one's preaching. The current inerrancy debate is no insignificant matter. Some think the whole debate about Bible inspiration is merely a matter of semantics. We quibble with words, they say. Most assuredly the issue is not merely semantic. The very life and health and future of the modern church are at stake. The outcome of the inerrancy debate is eternally important to the men and women, young people, and children who sit in our churches Sunday by Sunday.

Could the sparsity of good expository preachers be due to that lack of conviction about the Bible's accuracy and authority? The preacher is assigned the responsibility to preach the Word of God. Jesus commanded Simon Peter, "Feed my lambs" (John 21:15-17). Paul urged young Timothy, "Preach the word" (1 Tim. 4:2). To the elders of Ephesus Paul admonished, "Feed the church of God" (Acts 20:28). If the preacher's confidence in the power and authority of the Scriptures is shattered, the preacher will have no sense of urgency to preach the Bible.

G. Campbell Morgan is known as the Prince of Expositors. Perhaps you have read of his personal crisis concerning the authority of Scripture. Being influenced by some of the critical theories in his day that undermined the accuracy and authority of Scripture, Dr.

2. Merrill F. Unger, *Principles of Expository Preaching* (Grand Rapids: Zondervan, 1955), p. 18.

Morgan was plunged into a darkness of doubt. Then, setting aside all his books, he determined to discover for himself if the Bible was indeed what it claimed to be. The result was not merely that he found the Bible but, as he said, "The Bible found me." The result of that experience is a ministry that blessed two continents during his lifetime, and that, through his books, continues to bless preachers and Christians throughout the world.

Billy Graham faced a similar crisis in his young ministry. There came a time when he was not sure the Bible was indeed the Word of God. In a time of deep spiritual commitment, Dr. Graham committed himself to God and to the preaching of the Bible as God's Word to man. All of us have been moved by his piercing statement "The Bible says." The authority that flows from the preaching ministry of Billy Graham is impressive and gripping.

When Paul wrote to the believers in Thessalonica he said, "Our gospel came not unto you in word only, but also in power, and in the Holy Ghost, and in much assurance" (1 Thess. 1:5-6). That sense of authority is not a blessing to be minimized. Rather than submitting to the opinions of men and their ideas, the preacher can preach from a "Thus saith the Lord" stance. When the preacher preaches from that perspective the authority and power of the Word become prominent in his pulpit ministry. The preacher who preaches out of deep conviction that the Bible is God's living Word to man will discover that the power of God works mightily as he preaches.

The sense of preaching God's authoritative Word also involves a thrilling awareness of being a fellow laborer with God. Wonder and awe come to the preacher who realizes that God is using him in reaching men and in changing their lives. To be sure, one's convictions about the Word of God are vital.

Irving L. Jensen says, "Access to the inmost sanctuary of the Holy Scripture is granted only to those who come to worship."[3] The Bible is a miracle book. It is a miracle in its origin. W. E. Gladstone said, "The Bible is stamped with a specialty of origin, and an immeasurable distance separates it from all competitors."[4] Many years of careful study of the Bible have convinced me that the Bible is a book that man could not have written if he would and would not have

3. Irving L. Jensen, *Enjoy Your Bible* (Chicago: Moody, 1969), p. 27.
4. Ibid., p. 7.

written if he could. I am convinced of the inerrancy of Scripture for many reasons. One of the main reasons is that it speaks inerrantly about my own heart and life. The Bible tells me whence I came and whose I am.

This miracle book has survived through all the centuries. Diocletian, in A.D. 303, commanded that all the copies of the Bible be burned; yet the Bible still lives. The inscription on the monument to the Huguenots of Paris expresses the Bible's miraculous longevity succinctly, yet adequately: "Hammer away ye hostile hands; your hammers break; God's anvil stands."

The transmission of the Bible through thousands of copies into modern print is another miracle. Several years ago a soap slogan declared its product was "99 and 44/100 percent pure." The purity of the Bible text is even better than that. No other book of ancient literature has been exposed to similar processes of propagation, yet has maintained such accuracy of transmission. The accuracy of the Bible text is beyond question. Only the sovereign control of God through the centuries can account for that.

Views of Inspiration

Some regard the Bible as just one good book among many. My years of preaching the Bible Sunday after Sunday have convinced me that cannot be true. I have often wondered what would happen if I attempted to lecture from Shakespeare Sunday after Sunday. How long would it last? How many weeks would pass before I had lost my audience? In years of preaching I have seen weekly, continual preaching through books of the Bible fill churches to overflowing. No other book could draw crowds as has the Bible.

THE BIBLICAL VIEW

Suppose you were introduced to a man you had never previously met. You do not know who he is or where he is from. How would you determine what his background is? You might consult a skin expert. Let the dermatologist, on the basis of the man's skin, give us a scholarly guess as to where the man lives. Next, call in a hair expert;

he might be able to tell you the man's national origin. Other experts could give learned opinions as to who the man is and his homeland. You might indeed answer your questions about the man in that manner. There is a better way, however. If you really want to know about a man, the best way is to ask the man himself. And the best way to find out about the inspiration of the Bible is to let the Bible speak for itself.

Several passages of Scripture give the Bible's view concerning its own inspiration. Second Peter 1:21 says, "For the prophecy came not in old time by the will of man: but holy men of God spake as they were moved by the Holy Ghost." The picture is of men being borne along by the Holy Spirit, much as a sailboat would be borne along by the wind. The clear picture of the passage is that those men, chosen to write the inspired Word, did so superintended by the Holy Spirit. There is a dual authorship involved in Holy Scripture: the Holy Spirit is the divine author, and various men were the human authors. Acts 1:16 beautifully pictures this authorship: "Men and brethren, this Scripture must needs have been fulfilled, which the Holy Ghost by the mouth of David spake before concerning Judas."

The personalities of the Bible writers still come through clearly in their writings. One can see the burning sarcasm of Isaiah; the tender, earnest pathos of Jeremiah; the philosophical leanings of John; the sharp, crisp logic of Paul. Each of those Bible writers was truly a man with his own mind. Each man was as the individual pipe of a magnificent organ. Each pipe of the organ is so fashioned that it might give one particular note and not another. Yet each pipe is filled with the same breath. Even so, those holy men were fashioned by the circumstances of their lives and the genetic combination of their personalities to each give out his own note, yet all were filled by the breath of the divine Spirit.

Second Timothy 3:16 indicates the Bible is inspired in its totality. The verse clearly states: "All scripture is given by inspiration of God." This is plenary inspiration. All Scripture, the totality of Scripture, is inspired.

Inspiration extends to the words as well as the thoughts. Some hold a conceptual view of inspiration, maintaining that the thought patterns, but not the individual words, are inspired. How one might have thoughts apart from words has not been explained. First Corinthians 2:13 says, "Which things also we speak, not in the words which man's wisdom teacheth, but which [referring to the words] the Holy Ghost teacheth." The words the Holy Spirit teaches are clearly the words of Scripture. Our Lord taught that the smallest letter and even part of a letter are inspired of God. He said in Matthew 5:18: "For verily I say unto you, Till heaven and earth pass, one jot or one tittle shall in no wise pass from the law, till all be fulfilled." That is indeed a high view of inspiration. It is held by none other than our Lord Himself. If one is committed to the lordship of Jesus he must surely give careful attention to His view of Scripture.

The Bible also teaches the inerrancy of Holy Scripture. Jesus said in John 17:17: "Sanctify them through thy truth; thy word is truth." The Holy Spirit so overruled the human limitations of the Bible authors that what they wrote is without error. If we can grant the Spirit's power to overrule human limitation at any point, can we not then admit His superintendence over every matter given in Scripture? For that reason, one may intelligently hold there are no scientific errors, no historical errors, no prophetic errors in the Bible. If I cannot trust my Bible on those matters, how can I have confidence in Scripture on matters concerning my soul's salvation?

We are not obligated to clear away every difficulty in order to believe. Admittedly there are areas where we do not have final answers, but as new information becomes available to us many supposed difficulties evaporate. That is true especially in historical matters found in Scripture. Each new archaeological discovery seems to further vindicate the accuracy and integrity of the Bible. If we now have answers to questions that perplexed us in years gone by, may we not reasonably suppose that in the years ahead we will receive still further answers?

Inspiration is claimed only for the original manuscripts. That is often used as a reason to criticize the high view of inspiration. Many confidently say that we cannot maintain a view of accuracy for documents we have never seen. But although the original documents cannot be found, the correct text can be recovered with accuracy from many sources. Perhaps this simple illustration might explain the matter:

On January 1, 1863, President Lincoln set his name and seal on the proclamation which set four million slaves free. The proclamation was written on four pages of ordinary foolscap in the president's own handwriting. That document perished in the great Chicago Fire of 1871. Suppose some slave-owner should seize a former slave of his, challenge him to produce Lincoln's Proclamation as his charter of liberty, and say that if he did not produce the original, he would hold him still in slavery; what could the ex-slave do? He could not produce the original, for the original was destroyed by fire. Although he could not produce the original *document,* he could recover and produce the original *text.* How? By copies of the same in public documents; newspapers of the period; by translations of the text in French, German, and other languages; by quotations from the proclamation in speeches, periodicals and books. By comparing and combining all these, he could establish to the satisfaction of a court of law the original message which gave him liberty.[5]

Though we do not have the original scriptural *documents*, we are most confident that we have in the multiplicity of manuscripts available to us now the correct *text*. I know of no serious scholar who would challenge that.

I could not seriously give myself to the task of Bible exposition if I did not hold this high view of Scripture. I do not mean to question the sincerity or honesty of those who may hold lesser views. I merely appeal for earnest, prayerful thought about the matter. If there are doubts in a man's heart about the absolute accuracy and integrity of the Word, most likely he will have a difficult time doing word studies, fervently seeking to know what the text actually says, and yielding his personal life to its commands.

The preacher should know intimately the author of the Bible. Once a book that at first seemed rather dull and uninteresting to a young woman suddenly became a thrilling and exciting story. What made the difference? She met the author and fell in love with him! If the preacher has fallen in love with the Lord, he will love His Word. That love for the Bible and for the Lord will be conveyed enthusiastically to those who hear him preach.

5. George Henderson, *The Wonderful Word* (Edinburgh: B. McCall Barbour, n.d.), p. 13.

The Preacher's Devotional Life

Just as the scientist may lose God in his test tube, the preacher may lose God in his study. He may become so involved in the mechanics of sermon preparation that he loses his awareness of the presence of God in his personal life. It is urgent that the preacher develop a very strong devotional life. Many different names may be attached to this time. Some have called it the quiet time. Others may prefer "daily devotions." Whatever you call this time, be sure to have it!

Daily time for Bible study and prayer is the key to being an effective preacher. How can we possibly communicate the reality of God to those who listen to us preach unless we have been in God's presence ourselves? If we would speak effectively for God, we must first spend time alone with Him. I cannot emphasize the importance of this time with God too strongly, although many greatly gifted men do miss its importance. One may easily rationalize—the preacher spends a great deal of his time with the things of God; he reads his Bible in sermon preparation; he studies commentaries; he leads prayer meetings and prayer groups. He is constantly talking the language of Zion. But the accumulation of this "holy work" can dull the preacher's awareness of the need to be alone with God in his own personal life.

I enjoy reading biographies of great preachers. One characteristic common to all of them is a strong devotional life. Their preaching always gave evidence of a strong private communion with God. I have been blessed to know many of the great preachers of our day, and have talked with many of them about their devotional lives. Without exception each of them gives testimony to the essential place of personal devotions in his preaching and sermon preparation.

Many otherwise gifted men miss the mark at just this point. Aware of the great gifts they have, they assume those gifts will suffice. But God's gifts exercised in the energy of the flesh are a source of death, not life. Do not allow yourself to minimize the need to develop a sense of humble dependence upon God. We must have the strength that can come only from God. Such needed strength is derived as we wait before Him on our knees, before an open Bible.

Merrill F. Unger, discussing the importance of personal devotions in effective expository preaching, says, "It takes a long while for many otherwise able expositors to discover this simple fact. Others never realize it. As result their ministry is characterized by intellectuality rather than spirituality. The letter of Biblical truth is illuminated, but not properly combined with the Spirit and power of the Word."[6]

The importance of a personal devotional life was brought home to me during my freshman year in college. Since my call to preach at the age of sixteen, I had maintained a brief morning time for Bible reading and prayer. Upon my arrival at college, I immediately delved into my preparatory studies for the ministry. I was majoring in Bible, and my days were filled with reading many, many chapters from the Bible, sometimes as many as thirty chapters nightly. The next day I would be expected to take an examination on those chapters. In addition, I was studying Greek, philosophy, and additional liberal arts courses.

I found time to be at a premium. So I convinced myself I was reading the Bible as much as I needed. I failed to understand there is a difference between reading the Bible to take a test and reading God's Word to feed one's heart. I also had some brief prayer time. Frankly, my prayers primarily included urgent appeals to pass the examinations! As a result of my neglect of a daily devotional time, my heart became very cold to the things of God. I found myself becoming very critical and judgmental of others. On the outside, everything seemed fine. No one would have known I was far from God. On the inside, however, matters were quite different.

Through a citywide crusade preached by a lay speaker, I was awakened to the fact that my problem came from neglecting a daily quiet time. I asked God's forgiveness and reestablished my quiet time. Since then my daily devotional time has been the highlight of my Christian life. I cannot do without a daily time for Bible reading and prayer. On those rare times when I have been unable to begin my day thus, the day has not gone far until I am consciously aware of a poverty of spirit and a depletion in power.

I want to give some suggestions for establishing a daily devotional life. I promise you, such a time will be the power source of your entire ministry, especially your preaching.

6. Unger, p. 61.

BIBLE READING

What do you do in a daily devotion? Different preachers approach the subject in a variety of ways. Normally, I am up at 6:00 A.M. I go immediately to my study. My wife is kind enough to prepare my breakfast at that early hour. I eat only a small bowl of oatmeal and have a cup of coffee. I do this in my study. As I begin my day I have a brief prayer that God will speak to my heart, give me light, and make Himself real to me as I begin.

First of all, there is my Bible reading time. The Bible is most profitably read with some kind of system to guide you. Many different methods have been prepared. Let me share with you my own method. Each morning I read three chapters in the Old Testament, one chapter in the wisdom literature (Job—Song of Solomon), and three in the New Testament. That makes it possible for me to go completely through my Old Testament each year and through the New Testament several times in the year. I am not looking for sermons; I am listening for the voice of God to my personal life. Very often God gives me helpful insights for sermons, but that is not the purpose of the Bible reading time. I am just listening to His voice as I read His Word. I learn how much He loves me, what He has promised me, what He wants me to do. It is a very precious time. I am growing in the Lord during this time of Bible reading.

My Bible reading is more exciting at some times than at others, but I do not allow the presence or absence of excitement to deter me. God's Word is my daily nourishment. Whether I am excited about food or not does not affect my growth. I am looking now at my little finger. I realize there was a time, many years ago, when my little finger was only about one-third its present size. Because I have been eating food through the years, my little finger has grown. I cannot say I ever saw it grow; but, comparing the size now with the previous years, I know that it has. The same is true with Christian growth. As you feed upon the milk of the Word you grow (1 Pet. 2:2).

PRAYER

After I read my Bible I get on my knees for a time of prayer. When I read the Bible God speaks to me; when I pray I speak to God.

My prayer time has become increasingly meaningful to me. As I pray I simply talk to God as I would talk to you. Of course, I do not mean I talk to God with a sense of unjustified familiarity. But it is a very personal time. I begin by loving and adoring the Lord. I thank Him for my salvation, my call to the ministry, the opportunity of serving Him, and all the sources of gratitude that fill my heart on that particular morning. I have a genuine praise time.

Also, I make specific requests. I pray for each member of my family individually—my wife and each of my four children. I pray that God will bless their lives, and address particular problems they may be experiencing. I pray God will give my children Christian mates. I pray they will live for the Lord Jesus and serve Him.

Prayer for my church family is a prominent feature in my prayer time. I pray that sick members in the congregation will be healed. I pray for the members of our staff. I pray about specific prayer needs in our congregation. I get the people into my heart in this manner—I find I am better able to prepare sermons for my people if I am much in prayer for them. I pray for special events in the life of our church, and ask God to keep us on course in our soul-winning and Bible teaching ministries. During this time I discuss with the Lord the total life of our church.

In recent years I have spent a great deal of time praying for my preacher brethren. God has given me a great love for my fellow preachers. That love was instilled in me at an early age. I pray specifically for personal friends, asking the Lord to bless their ministries. This part of my prayer time is very precious to me. I have been strengthened and encouraged to know my preacher friends are praying for me. I am grateful to have the opportunity to pray for them in return.

Generally my devotion time lasts about forty-five minutes, but there is no hard and fast rule. Take whatever time you need to get your life in touch with God for the day through His Word and prayer. Time spent in this manner will not take away from specific sermon preparation.

From time to time I have found it helpful to use devotional guides. Some books have been especially helpful to me in developing my spiritual life. For many years I have started each year reading one chapter each morning in E. M. Bounds's classic *Power Through*

Prayer. I would urge every preacher to read this little book on prayer. Bounds's book has done more to help me develop my own prayer life than anything I have ever read. Bounds's emphasis on prayer seems to help me at the beginning of the year. Each reading impresses upon me afresh the role prayer plays in my ministry.

Several years ago in my devotion time I read through Ruth Paxson's three-volume work *Life on the Highest Plane.* This is a very lengthy work dealing with the spiritual life. You might want to take a page or two a day and read through it as part of your daily devotional time. James Gilchrist Lawson's *Deeper Experiences of Famous Christians* is another helpful volume. It gives the experiences of many great Christians who learned to walk with God in a deeper spiritual experience, and I have found it helpful to me as I have grown in the Lord. Raymond Edman's *They Found the Secret* is a similar, smaller volume. His book would be helpful to you as well.

There are several other books on prayer that might help to stimulate your devotional life. Andrew Murray has many helpful volumes. *With Christ in the School of Prayer* is a good one to read one chapter a day. John R. Rice wrote a classic on prayer entitled *Prayer: Asking and Receiving.* The preacher will find great encouragement in Dr. Rice's book. *The Kneeling Christian* (author unknown) is another book that has blessed me in my personal prayer life. These books have served to challenge me to pray and to help me to properly channel my prayers.

I have found the books of A. W. Tozer very helpful. Tozer's book *The Pursuit of God* is invaluable in developing the devotional life. Let me urge you to read some of Tozer's books. They will bless you and will strengthen your devotional life.

There are some daily guides that can provide help to the preacher in his personal devotional life. *Our Daily Bread, The Daily Walk,* and the devotional books of Mrs. Charles Cowman are all very good. I have used these only in a limited way. For me the reading of the Bible serves as my primary devotional material. But in beginning your devotional life you might find one of these guides beneficial to you. Do whatever you have to do to begin and nurture the devotional time.

I do not have words to express to you what the devotional time can mean. Over and over again I have left my knees with the joy of the Lord bursting from my heart. The tone of the day is set. I am ready to give myself to sermon preparation. I have met with the Lord! My soul has basked in the sunshine of His love! I am right with Him. I am now ready to prepare sermons to minister to the people. This daily time keeps my heart free of unconfessed sin. I am conscious again of the main business. I am now ready to be the preacher God called me to be.

I would not attempt to serve as a pastor or prepare sermons for preaching without a daily devotional time. This is without doubt the lifeline of my ministry. Whatever success I may have experienced in the ministry I attribute to this daily contact with God. Stephen Olford has written a helpful little booklet on the devotional time entitled *Manna in the Morning*. The devotional time is exactly that to me— manna for my hungry soul at the beginning of the day.

The Preacher's Intellectual Development

The preacher must be a student. Because he is called upon to preach the Word of God to others he must prepare himself intellec-tually to the fullest extent of his abilities. No preacher should be satisfied to use only bits and pieces of the intellectual abilities with which God has blessed him. Of course, one may be a preacher of unusual gifts and bring tremendous blessing without formal education. Many of the great men of God through the ages had very little formal training. John Bunyan, Charles Spurgeon, and G. Campbell Morgan were greatly gifted preachers who had very little training in formal schools. The Bible says Peter and John were "unlearned and ignorant men" (Acts 4:13). That means they never attended the school of the rabbis—yet who can doubt the spiritual power that flowed from their ministries? Nevertheless, we may be confident all of these men would have urged the would-be preacher to take advantage of every possible means to train himself.

FORMAL TRAINING

I am grateful to God for the formal training I have received, and I wish I could have had more. I have not looked upon my college and seminary training as a means to an end. Rather, I have viewed it as an opportunity to hone the gifts God has given to me.

The preacher will benefit from a broad, general education. Comprehensive studies in the arts and sciences will prove invaluable. He should study psychology, history, biology, and sociology. Truth is truth, wherever one may find it. The preacher need not fear God's truth even when it is found in what may be considered a secular source. I would urge the young men who are reading this book to take advantage of every opportunity to receive a thorough liberal arts education. It provides the preacher with a wonderful intellectual and cultural background for his preaching, and will prove invaluable to him in years to come. (As I look back on my own studies, I wish I had applied myself more.) Academic training will provide a storehouse of useful information for preaching: a broader understanding of life will be gained, and illustrations and methods for applying biblical truth to life will flow from your previous training as the years go by.

One of the most encouraging developments in my day has been the rise of theologically sound Bible colleges. Because of them thousands of young men have been able to receive excellent Bible training. But let me give one word of caution: a Bible college may deprive the preacher of the broadness needed in his training. That does not have to be the case, for more and more those who lead and teach in Bible colleges are urging their young students to widen their scope of outside reading. Also increasingly, Bible colleges are providing in their curricula courses covering a wide range of subjects. Bible college catalogs are now frequently offering selected studies in literature, philosophy, psychology, and science. I am merely urging that the Bible college-trained preacher not confine himself to biblical and theological studies.

The preacher should also acquire as much specific education in the area of theology and Bible as he possibly can. Herein is the value of Bible college and seminary training. There is tremendous value in acquiring a knowledge of the original languages. By all means the preacher should study Hebrew and Greek. Many language helps are available today. The preacher with no knowledge of the languages can get much help from books. Such volumes as W. E. Vine's *Expository Dictionary of New Testament Words* and A. T. Robertson's *Word Pictures in the New Testament* can be greatly beneficial, but they leave the preacher entirely dependent upon secondary sources. There is something fresh and exciting about going to the original to find the truth for yourself. There is a confidence and sense of authority that comes to your study. I am not saying the preacher cannot preach effectively without a knowledge of languages, but I am suggesting there is a great advantage to him if he can read Hebrew and Greek. I would urge those who have had introductory courses in the languages to continue to pursue those studies. I have found my own ministry greatly enhanced through a study of Greek syntax and word origins through the years. My preaching has benefited enormously.

The preacher should be trained in theology, both systematic and biblical. Systematic theology has value in that the preacher is given a framework for his understanding of Bible doctrines. Biblical theology will make him aware that he is dealing with the very mind of God in the Holy Scriptures. Biblical theology will help the preacher avoid the danger of putting all Bible doctrine in neat little compartments.

Formal study in the area of Bible interpretation is helpful. As the preacher learns proper principles of Scripture interpretation, he will learn to avoid "off the wall" interpretations. He will learn the importance of studying Scripture in context. Studying Bible interpretation will make the preacher aware of the different interpretations offered for controversial passages. That will help him avoid enslaving himself to any man's particular system of interpretation. This area of study will teach him to be aware of the main interpretations that have been made through the years.

In formal training the preacher can also get help in the areas of sermon preparation and delivery. These are areas where new and exciting work is being done. We are on the threshold of fascinating insights in matters of biblical exegesis and sermonic composition. In the days ahead new and helpful materials will be available to the preacher student. The wise man will want to avail himself of these innovative new tools.

PASTORAL EXAMPLE

Another facet of the preacher's intellectual preparation needs consideration. The church where the young preacher is called to the ministry plays a crucial role in his preparation. A strong, warm, Bible-preaching church creates an atmosphere conducive to launching the young preacher toward a successful ministry. A cold, skeptical, liberal church may greatly cripple a young preacher as he attempts his first steps in the ministry. The pastor should be a positive role model for the budding young man of God. To sit under the ministry of a good, faithful, expository pastor gives a young man a head start in his ministry. I have spent much time with the young men in my churches who have been called to preach. The pastor can train them, encourage them, and point them to a good choice for their formal schooling.

I hasten to say again, I am merely encouraging young preachers to prepare themselves intellectually to the fullest extent of their abilities. I am in no way suggesting that formal training is the sine qua non of preaching effectiveness. I am just saying, get all the education you possibly can.

BE A STUDENT

Regardless of one's past intellectual training, the preacher should spend all the days of his ministry studying and preparing himself to preach. Every day should be a search for general materials for preaching. Study in as many areas as possible. Do your best to keep abreast of the times. Read a good newspaper every day. I have recently found the national paper *USA Today* a very helpful way to keep up with what is going on in the world. If you cannot read many books, study book reviews. Be aware of what is going on in the world of literature, in the motion picture industry, and on television. You do not have to watch everything on television. Normally, good reviews are available in the papers. Read biography. Read good novels. Stretch your mental capacities. You will be amazed how this will help you in your sermon preparation and also in your sermon delivery.

Be a student of preaching throughout your ministry. Study the lives of the great preachers. Warren Wiersbe's book *Walking with the Giants* is very helpful in getting acquainted with some of the great preachers of the past. I try regularly to read a book on some aspect of preaching. Be constantly studying your work. Look for new ways to go about your task of preaching. Talk with other preachers. Glean from them their methods of sermon preparation.

The preacher's entire life is a process of intellectually preparing himself to preach. You should bring your finest intellectual efforts to your sermon preparation. Koller says it quite well: "A preacher must not preach out of the fullness of his heart and the emptiness of his head."[7]

The Preacher in the Study

The time has come to go into the study. We are interested at this point in understanding just what the preacher does there. Without trying to be ridiculous let me say that the preacher must go into his study prepared to study. If this seems trite to you, a few years of sermon preparation will change your mind. The easiest thing in the world for a preacher to do is to waste time under the impression he is studying. The preacher faces a constant danger of laziness within his study walls. Most preachers are able to plan and organize their own daily schedules, but the preacher may waste his hours in the study. Many have not developed good habits of study through the years. Just because you are sitting at your desk for a period of hours, do not suppose this guarantees you are actually studying.

A story is told of the young preacher who did not study as he should. He frequently bragged to his deacons that his messages were prepared between the time he left his pastorium in the morning and the time he arrived at the door of the church. No wonder his deacons bought him a new home five miles away![8] Altogether too much poor preaching is due to "suppressed perspiration." R. G. Lee used to say, "You can't live on skim milk during the week and preach cream on Sunday."

THE DISCIPLINE OF STUDY

The preacher must take whatever steps necessary to develop the discipline of study. Perhaps every preacher should read a book on time management. Some booklets on how to study are available at high schools and colleges. Learn how to discipline your time. For many years I have been arranging my weekly morning study times in a very definite manner. On Monday morning I prepare a half sheet of paper divided into the days of the week. On the bottom of the page I put down what my study requirements are for the week. For instance,

7. Charles W. Koller, *Expository Preaching Without Notes* (Grand Rapids: Baker, 1962), p. 44.
8. John R.W. Stott, *Between Two Worlds* (Grand Rapids: Eerdmans, 1982), p. 211.

for the week I may have a Sunday morning and Sunday evening message to prepare. In addition to this, I may need to prepare a message to be delivered in an outside speaking engagement. Also, I may be called upon to preach at some function in our church besides the normal services. Each of these preaching opportunities is put down. Then, I arrange on a daily basis the time I will spend on each preparation. I may set aside two hours on Monday morning for my Sunday morning message. I may schedule one hour for my Sunday night message. In addition, I may schedule another hour for one of the other speaking engagements. This does not mean I will necessarily follow to the minute the schedule I have prepared. I am simply preparing some kind of time structure for each day. Arranging a schedule will be helpful to you as you prepare to study each day.

LOCATION

Where will the preacher's study be located? Often the structure of the preacher's particular church will be determinative in this matter. Most likely the congregation will provide a study at the church. For many years I studied at the room provided by the churches where I served. In more recent years I have moved my study home. Find an extra room at your house. Maybe even use your basement or attic. Try to have your study in a secluded place. If at all possible, have your study away from the traffic flow. There are advantages to a study at home. You will be away from the activities at the church. A preacher finds study extremely difficult at the church when much activity is going on. In my own experience, well-thinking members of the congregation would inevitably come by to visit for a few moments, which stretched into an hour or more. What finally convinced me to move my study home was the morning a member dropped by to see me. He said "Well, preacher, since I am retired now, I have a lot of time on my hands. I didn't figure you had anything to do this morning, so I thought I would drop by to see you!"

The move was the best one I ever made. My wife is able to screen my calls for me. When I moved my study home I explained to the people what I was doing. I told them I wanted to be the best possible preacher for them I could be. I wanted to faithfully preach God's Word to them. In order for me to do so, I needed uninterrupted study time. The people were understanding and patient. In a matter of just a few months they were adjusted to this change. The obvious improvement in the pulpit gave them an understanding of the value of the study away from the church.

I have been studying in the mornings for most of the years of my ministry. The mornings seem to be the best time for me. I begin my study time around 6:00 A.M., including my daily devotional time. I normally study until 11:00 A.M., I do this five mornings each week. I function best in the morning. But Martin Lloyd-Jones is correct when he says there are no universal rules about the time of study. Each man must know himself. I have friends who seem to do best at night. Each man's body will differ in these matters.[9]

The morning hours of study have some definite advantages. The afternoon hours are good for tending to administrative matters of the church. The evening time needs to be spent with the wife and children as much as possible. Normally, the children will be in school during the morning hours. This will enable the preacher to have quiet time then for study. If you have small, preschool children, this may not work for you for a few years. But as they grow older you will be able to block out these morning hours for your study time.

Some men use an out-of-the-way place at the church for their studies. I was recently in a very fine study of one of our best preachers. His study is located on an out-of-the-way hall in the church complex. The door is almost unnoticeable. On the inside my preacher friend has a very large, commodious study. He does an excellent job of sermon preparation in this obscure place.

I am fortunate to have an additional study at church away from the main church offices. This is a helpful place to go at odd times for some extra study. I can go there without being worried with a telephone or with the chatter that goes on around a church office. Whether at home or at church, find the best place for your study.

TOOLS

Several items are important in the place of your study. A good desk is needed. See that you have plenty of shelves for your books.

---

9. D. Martyn Lloyd-Jones, *Preaching and Preachers* (Grand Rapids: Zondervan, 1971), p. 167.

Make the lighting of the room the best possible. The walls should be thick enough to keep out noises. I realize not all circumstances can be ideal in these matters. Do your best to make your room as conducive to good study as you possibly can.

Let me suggest to you several important tools. Buy an inexpensive giant-print Bible. Be sure it is giant print. Billy Graham says the print in many Bibles is so small it should be called "devil's print." I keep a giant-print King James Version Bible on my study desk at all times. This is the Bible I use for beginning my Bible study and sermon preparation. I also keep handy other translations. The *New American Standard Bible* is a good one. The newer *New International Version* is also good. Several paraphrases can give additional insights. You will find *The Living Bible* can give you a new understanding of a familiar passage from time to time. You do not have to endorse everything in a paraphrase to be helped. J. B. Phillips's *Paraphrase of the New Testament* is one of the best. Many times I have turned to Phillips with profit. There are several multitranslation volumes available. It might be helpful to purchase one of those. This will enable you to see at a glance what the major translators have done on a particular verse.

Several other items will be helpful tools. A good Bible concordance is important. *Robert Young's Analytical Concordance to the Bible* is good. I have been using *Strong's Concordance* for several years. An exhaustive concordance will enable you to search out each word in a particular verse. I find this helpful in doing cross-reference work on a particular passage. Study a word all the way through the Bible. A good concordance is invaluable in this kind of study. Get a Bible atlas. Understanding of the geography of the Bible lands is beneficial. Several good Bible atlases are available.

Dictionaries are an important part of your study. If you do not understand the meaning of a word, how can you understand the verse where the word is used? Study your English dictionary. I have found a dictionary of synonyms to be useful from time to time. This will give you variety in the words you use in your sermons. A Bible dictionary is an essential tool of study. *Zondervan Pictorial Bible Dictionary* is one of the better newer works. If you prefer a more extensive dictionary, the *International Standard Bible Encyclopedia* is the best one with which I am familiar. Bible dictionaries give you ready information about Bible terms, places, and people. You will use your Bible dictionary frequently.

Other tools of study should include several volumes that will help your study of Bible words. W. E. Vine's *Expository Dictionary of New Testament Words* is a good multivolume set of word studies. Some new books on Hebrew word studies are good. You might like to purchase *Old Testament Word Studies* by William Wilson.

More tools to help the preacher in his study are available now than ever before. The wise preacher will invest in several helpful volumes. Let me recommend some books I frequently use as reference works. *The Treasure of Scripture Knowledge* (Revell) is good. *Figures of Speech Used in the Bible,* by E. W. Bullinger, is invaluable. *The Emphasized Bible,* by Joseph Bryant Rotherham, will provide additional insights. There are many more. Purchase books that will assist you throughout your preaching ministry.

What should the preacher do about commentaries? Many large sets of commentaries are available. I have many in my personal library. Quite frankly, most of them are of very little use to me. A better way is to buy individual books by good expositors. When I am preaching on the book of Romans, for instance, I try to find the best volumes available on Romans. No one man is good on every book of the Bible. Some individual commentaries are classics. H. A. Ironside's book *In the Heavenlies,* a commentary on Ephesians, is a masterpiece. His commentary on Acts was a disappointment. Find the best books on the particular book from which you are preaching. Other preachers will give you suggestions. Survey the shelves of the bookstores. Look for booklists provided by seminaries and in volumes on preaching. Find the very best written on your particular preaching assignment. I don't know who said it first, but I certainly agree with the statement: "I milk a lot of cows, but I make my own butter." Draw all you can from the works of gifted men.

In addition to your scheduled time for study, find all the additional time you can. If you can snatch an extra hour in the afternoon, do it. Read everything you can get your hands on. Francis Bacon said, "Reading maketh a full man." Alexander Whyte, a Scottish minister, advised, "Sell your shirt and buy books."[10] Be constantly building a

10. William Evans, *How to Prepare Sermons* (Chicago: Moody, 1964), p. 31.

good library. Though you will keep most of your books in your study, you will want to have books at other places. Have a good book in your church office. Keep a book at bedside. When you travel, throw a good book into your suitcase. Strive for good variety in your reading matter. Everything you read will be helpful information for your sermons.

A WORD OF CAUTION

Let me give you a word of caution about your study. All theory and no experience makes for an unreal preacher. Do not cloister yourself away in your study and fail to relate to the outside world. The preacher who comes from his ivory tower to the pulpit on Sunday morning will lack the ring of reality in what he has to say. Constantly test your studies in the crucible of daily life. Bounce your ideas off your wife, your children, your church members, and your peers. They will correct much of your faulty, idealistic thinking.

A good preacher will continue to be a student throughout his life. Spurgeon said, "He who has ceased to learn has ceased to teach. He who no longer sows in the study will no more reap in the pulpit."[11] Continue to study, and you will continue to be fresh and interesting. As you study you will find messages springing from your soul like water bubbling from a fountain. I have heard many preachers express regret that they studied so little in their lives. Donald Grey Barnhouse said, "If I had only three years to serve the Lord, I would spend two of them studying and preparing."[12] The preacher who studies will never lack something to say. If you study, the people will know it and be appreciative. If you do not study, they will know you do not very, very soon. The workman not ashamed must be a workman who studies.

The Importance of Physical Fitness

Americans are getting into shape! Everywhere you go now you see men and women in jogging gear, laboriously running alongside the roads. In the last several years there has been a renewed interest

11. Stott, p. 180.
12. Ibid., p. 181.

in good health. Millions of Americans are pursuing various forms of exercise. Jogging has become very popular. Health spas, exercise rooms, tennis courts, and other fitness facilities are doing a booming business all over the country. There is a proliferation of books on the subject of good physical conditioning. People are more conscious of their eating habits than ever before. Men as well as women are counting calories, pushing away from the table, and getting their weight down where it should be. Personally I am encouraged by this emphasis on physical conditioning. A healthier society will result. Healthier people should be a happier people.

This new interest on the body has a good Bible foundation. The Bible teaches the sacredness of the body. The believer's body is the temple of the Holy Spirit. The well-instructed believer understands the need to keep the temple in good shape. The better we care for our bodies, the better we should be able to serve our Lord. Christians should be very concerned about physical fitness, not for some of the reason others hold, but for reasons grounded in sound Bible teaching.

Physical fitness is a neglected area for many preachers. Too often the preacher is so involved in the Lord's work and the myriad activities at his church that he does not take adequate time to tend to the needs of his body. Some preachers may minimize the importance of physical fitness. One should not waste time in physical exercise or other forms of recreation. But wise is the preacher who will spend some time keeping his body in good condition. The preacher does not have to become an amateur athlete to attend to his physical needs. He will greatly benefit his ministry by engaging in some minimium form of exercising.

EXERCISE

Experience proves that if you do not find time for exercise you will have to find time for illness. I heard someone say several years ago that the body and the soul live so close together they catch one another's diseases. Modern physiology bears out this statement. You cannot benefit one part of your life without benefiting the whole. God intends his preachers to have sound minds *and* healthy bodies. Several essentials are necessary for the preacher's good health—fresh air, exercise, good food, and rest.

As we consider the subject of sermon preparation we have already seen many, many hours of your time each day must be spent in study. Most of those hours will be spent in intensive mental labor. This is the most tiring form of work. One may bounce back from strenuous forms of physical work in a relatively short time. To recover from mental labor quickly is not so easy. For this reason, the preacher needs to plan definite blocks of time for physical exercise.

Several years ago I found myself tired without being able to get rested. I woke up each morning feeling as if I had not slept. I was tired all the time. I decided to go to a doctor for a checkup. In the course of his examination he found nothing physically wrong with me. When he asked me what kind of exercise program I followed I replied that I had none. During my high school and college days I participated in all forms of sports. I was extremely active physically. For about ten years I had let my physical exercise go completely. The doctor instructed me to start some form of exercise. At this point I took up jogging. What miserable drudgery! The first time or two I tried jogging, I thought I was going to die. But I kept on jogging. In a matter of a few weeks my stamina was noticeably improved. I began to feel much better. I was resting better at night. In a few weeks I lost nine pounds. I had more stamina and energy than I had had in years. I have continued jogging to this day. I still cannot say I enjoy jogging, but I do enjoy the positive benefits I derive from it. I try to jog about thirty minutes a day, three days a week. This gives me a good, vigorous workout.

Jogging may not be for you. Other forms of exercise are just as good or even better. Swimming is a very good form of exercise. Basketball gives you the benefit of a strenuous workout, plus the enjoyment of being with others. Some men like racqetball or golf. (Don't ride the golf carts!) It doesn't matter what you do—just do something! Let me caution you to have a physical before you begin. Be sure the doctor gives you permission to do whatever you decide to do. Even those who are in poor condition physically can probably begin to walk. Walking is a good opportunity for the preacher to be with his wife. Why don't you and your wife begin walking together?

The time you spend getting exercise will not be wasted time. You will be more productive in your working hours because you take a few minutes each week for physical exercise. You will be able to think more clearly and will find your creative powers heightened.

PROPER EATING

Eating correctly helps your physical well being. The preacher needs to keep his weight under control. I know this is not easy to do. I have a constant battle to keep my weight where it should be. I count calories all the time. A good, balanced diet, including all the daily requirements from the various food groups, should keep your weight where you desire. Leave off in-between meal snacking. Avoid eating late at night. Eat only a minimum of sweets and bread. Cut down on your sugar intake. This will be very helpful to your throat as well. Sugar and milk have a tendency to form mucus. This can give you difficulties with your speaking voice. Eat plenty of green, leafy vegetables. Be sure you have an adequate intake of bulk. You don't have to become a health-food nut. Just give attention to proper eating. This will not only be good for your physical well-being; good weight control is also a positive testimony. How can we tell others Christ can give them power over drugs and alcohol when we seem to have no control over our eating habits? I know that hurts, brethren, but we know it is the truth.

REST

Most preachers I know do not get enough rest. My wife says I am a night owl. She is correct. I seem to really come alive in the late night hours. I have always been this way. I find it hard to get up early in the morning, though, if I stay up late at night. I have been consciously trying to go to bed earlier. The effort is paying off.

Especially does the preacher need to get adequate rest on Saturdays. I have recently begun to take off on Saturdays. I relax my mind completely. Most of the day is spent doing what I would like to do. I run in the morning, followed by a leisurely breakfast. My wife and I eat together at noon. This is a good time for us to be together. We have opportunity to discuss matters relating to our household. This is also an opportunity to communicate about our children. I do very little thinking about my Sunday sermon. On Saturday night I go into my study for a brief time to go over my message. I try to saturate my heart and soul with the content of my sermon. Time is spent in prayer, talking to the Lord about my message. Then I go to bed for a good night's rest. When Sunday morning comes I am rested and ready.

I am finding increasingly that a prepared body helps one deliver a prepared sermon. The body is the vehicle God uses to communicate His Word to men. Keep your body in good condition. Make your body a finely honed tool for God.

A story about the apostle John says that a young hunter at Ephesus, returning from the chase with an unstrung bow in his hand, entered John's house. To his amazement he found the beloved John engaged in playing with a tame dove. The young man showed his astonishment that the apostle should be so lightly employed. John, looking gently at him, asked him why he carried his bow unstrung in his hand. The young man replied that it was only in this way that it would retain its elasticity. Even so, said John, mind and body will not retain their elasticity or usefulness unless they are at times unstrung. Prolonged tension destroys the power of mind and body.   Even if fictitious, this story aptly illustrates the importance of physical recreation. Spend time on physical fitness. Such effort will improve the time you spend on sermon preparation.

Preparing the People

I am going to assume you have decided by now to begin the expository method of preaching. You are going to take a book of the Bible and preach consecutively through that book. Mentally, you are ready to go. Another matter of preparation must be considered at this juncture. Your congregation may have never heard this kind of preaching. Probably through the years they have been fed a regular diet of topical preaching. Unless your people have been blessed with a Bible expositor for a pastor, you may be the first preacher they have ever heard who will actually preach what the Bible says.

A NEW METHOD

This will involve an adjustment on the part of your people. Expository sermons will be different kinds of sermons to them. They may not even bring their Bibles to the services. You will have to train them to do so. You can do this by asking them at the beginning of your message if they have their Bibles. After doing this for a period of time, along with your preaching paragraph by paragraph through Bible books, the people will get in the habit of bringing Bibles with them. It is really thrilling to see a congregation trained to bring the Word of God to the services. There is no sweeter sound than the rustling of the leaves as you announce your Scripture for the sermon.

When a congregation has been accustomed to topical preaching, for a period of time expository preaching might not seem as thrilling to them. In later sections of this book I am going to share with you some methods to use to make expository preaching a most thrilling and exciting experience. But at the outset, the difference in method may be a radical change for them. I remember when I changed to the expository method in the middle of a pastorate. The people were fine people. For several years I had been going from topic to topic. When I started preaching through books of the Bible they were unaccustomed to the method. For a few weeks they were not on my wavelength. Very soon, however, they made the adjustment. When they caught on, they were completely hooked!

This has always been my experience. Once a congregation gets accustomed to book-by-book expository preaching they will never again be satisfied with another method. You will ruin them for life! They will complain when they hear anything else. I assure you that you will always have an audience when you use the expository method.

CHOOSING A BOOK

Assuming you are ready to begin the expository method, which book do you use as your beginning book? Let me give three suggestions. Choose a book carefully. One of the reasons I took several years to get into the expository method was an unfortunate experience in my first pastorate. My home pastor preached through books of the Bible. I really enjoyed hearing that method. In my first rural church I decided I would do this, too. However, I was an eighteen-year-old boy. Only one book beside the Bible did I own. I had never done more than speak to a few youth gatherings. I decided to begin a series of messages through the book of Romans. I had no commentaries on Romans. All I had was a Bible and an eager heart. The first week I read and read and reread Romans 1. I struggled, but a twenty-minute message was prepared from the first chapter. The next week was harder. To get something to say from the second chapter was all I could do. Those sixteen weeks, preparing one message per chapter through Romans, were the most miserable of my life. I was scared away from book-by-book preaching for many years. I tell you this to urge you to choose the book carefully. Why not begin with a book that is relatively simple and comparatively short? Do not start with the book of Revelation or Ezekiel! I suggest you choose a practical book rather than a doctrinal one. Begin with the book of James. James has only five chapters and abounds with practical application to today's world. Or, you might want to use the book of Philippians. Philippians has four chapters. There are few doctrinal nuts to crack. If you get in trouble, with only four chapters you can exit in a month! Choose a book carefully.

Choose your book according to need. Ask yourself, What do the people need? As you study your congregation you will see many areas where they need good Bible teaching and admonition. Find a Bible book that addresses those needs. As I have previously suggested, this has the advantage of allowing you to preach to the problems of your people without singling out individuals. As you proceed through a book of the Bible the people will expect you to interpret and apply the book as its stands.

Select a book prayerfully. Ask God to lead you. Surely if God can lead you to prepare one message, He can lead you to prepare a series of messages from a book in the Bible. Go to God in prayer. Find the book He wants you to use. The Lord will direct you. You can be confident of His guidance in this matter.

As you move through the book you will be thrilled to see God work. Needs you never dreamed would surface in the lives of your people will be answered by the passage of Scripture from which you are preaching.

THE INTRODUCTORY SERMON

The introductory sermon in a Bible book series is very important. This message helps prepare the people for the entire series. The pace is set for all the messages. Sometimes a birds-eye view of the book is a good way to begin. Arouse as much interest as possible in the book. Whet their appetites. Do not give the entire message of the book in the first sermon. Throw in just enough tidbits of information to create a sense of anticipation on the part of your people.

A new adventure in Bible study with your people will be yours. As they move through a portion of God's Word with you, both of you will be caught up in the awareness that you are coming in contact with the very mind of God. You will discover God is alive and is speaking in your day. The people to whom you introduce the expository method will rise up and call you blessed.

3

The Process of Exposition

We now come to the crucial stage in the process of sermon preparation—Bible exposition. In some ways this is the most difficult and yet in every way the most fascinating step in the entire process of sermonic work. Exposition is the fundamental step in preparing an expository sermon.

Charles W. Koller has given what he calls a basic pattern toward the preparation of an expository sermon. The pattern consists of three stages: First, there is the analysis. The purpose is to discover in the passage the basic content and progression of thought.

Second is exposition. The analysis has to be amplified and enlarged by interpretation and illustration.

Third is the sermon itself. The expository sermon, based upon careful analysis and exposition, takes the material, arranges the content into logical order, makes practical application to the lives of the people, is properly illustrated, then drives the message home.[1]

Our approach to expository sermon preparation will be different from Koller's approach in some aspects. We will spend a great deal of time considering the whole process of analyzing a passage of Scripture in preparing an expository sermon.

Many different approaches have been proposed. Kaiser gives the seven steps in the analysis of a passage as arranged by Victor Paul Furnish: First, formulate the main points of the passage. Discover from the passage itself the main points. Second, either note what is

1. Charles W. Koller, *Expository Preaching Without Notes* (Grand Rapids: Baker, 1962), pp. 20-22.

problematical in the passage or compare various translations to see if there is any major disagreement. Third, identify key words or concepts found in the passage. Fourth, list any historical, literary, or theological problems that are apparent in the text. Fifth, prepare a tentative outline for the passage in keeping with its overall context. Sixth, refer to parallel Bible passages or other related literature where ideas similar to the ones found in the passage appear. Seventh, record in note form whatever wider implications the passage may contain.[2]

I prefer to simplify my discussion of the process of exposition as much as possible. I am going to give you the relatively simple process I follow in the exposition of a Bible passage. I am interested in the matter of analysis. My concern is to dissect a Scripture passage into its parts. I want to take the passage apart. My aim at this point in preparation is to "pick to pieces" the passage of Scripture.

Perhaps several illustrations will assist your understanding of the process of exposition I follow. Imagine, for instance, a passage of Scripture to be a block of wood before you. Pick up the block of wood and turn it from side to side, over and over. Examine the block of wood carefully. Upon close examination you will find certain natural divisions in the block. When the natural divisions are found, crack the block of wood at those places. Perhaps there are three natural divisions in the wood. Crack the block into those three sections. This is what I do with a passage of Scripture.

This approach may be followed with an entire book of the Bible, such as Romans. A careful study of the sixteen chapters of Romans will reveal there are three main divisions. The first eight chapters group together. Chapters 9 through 11 are the second group. The last five chapters (12-16) go together. Divide the book of Romans into these main parts. Then, label each of these divisions. The first eight chapters may be labeled *doctrinal*. The second division, chapters 9-11, may be labeled *parenthetical*. The third division, chapters 12-16, may be labeled *practical*. This gives us a neat, simple analysis of the entire book of Romans. Now back to our block of wood. Take one of the smaller sections. Look again at the section to find the natural divisions. Examine carefully Romans 1-8. Look for the natural divisions of subject and thought patterns found in those eight chapters.

2. Walter C. Kaiser, Jr., *Toward an Exegetical Theology* (Grand Rapids: Baker, 1981), p. 43.

Again, crack your block of wood into those smaller divisions. In Romans 1-8 we find three major subdivisions. These may be labeled *sin* (chap. 1-3), *salvation* (chap. 3-5), and *sanctification* (chap. 6-8). Each of those subdivisions may be broken down as well. When the process is over our block of wood is now in neat piles of kindling.

Another way to explain the process of analysis is by means of an exploded diagram. In auto supply stores, exploded diagrams of automobile motors may be found. These exploded diagrams show each part of the motor separately and as it fits with the motor. Each is labeled. Look upon your Scripture passage as an exploded diagram. As you analyze the passage, explode the whole into constituent parts. Now label each part. This process of analysis gives you an overall view of the contents of a Scripture passage.

What we are interested in is exegesis. Exegesis means to explain the meaning of a Scripture passage. This involves leading out of the passage what the passage actually says. John 1:18 says, "No man hath seen God at any time; the only begotten Son, which is in the bosom of the Father, he hath declared [exegeted] him."

Our interest is exegesis, not eisegesis. Exegesis explains what the passage says. Eisegesis reads a preferred meaning into the passage. An interpretation is imposed upon the passage. This is basically the difference between the deductive and the inductive method. Deduction is a reasoning from the general to the particular. Induction is the process of inference by which we arrive at a more general truth from a particular set of facts. Deduction involves inferring a specific fact or truth from a more general one. Induction is concerned about collating, analyzing, observing everything in the passage as it relates to the subject being treated.[3] The preacher who gives himself to expository sermon preparation must be interested primarily in the inductive method. This is the only appropriate procedure if one is to arrive at what God has actually revealed on any particular subject. We are not interested in what we think about a subject. We are very much interested to know what God says about the subject.

As we analyze a passage we are concerned to discover several matters. We want to find the structural pattern. We are interested in the main, unifying theme. We also want to know what applications

3. Merrill F. Unger, *Principles of Expository Preaching* (Grand Rapids: Zondervan, 1955), pp. 98, 107.

may be made from the passage to our lives. Our desire is to discover timeless truths. Should no timeless truths be specifically expressed, we shall look for those that may be implied.

The analysis of the passage is the starting point for the preacher. The preacher must prayerfully, earnestly, diligently, painstakingly read the passage. He must find out what the passage means. He must discover what the passage has to say to him and to his people.

To make this process of exposition as simple as possible I want to give you the threefold process I follow in my expository work. I am indebted to Irving L. Jensen for this helpful approach to exposition: investigation, interpretation, and application.

Investigation

Investigation answers the question, What does the Scripture passage really say? This is the fundamental step in the process of Scripture exposition. We cannot determine what Scripture means until we know what Scripture says. There is only one way to determine this—read the passage.

We will assume at this point that the Bible book has been selected. After prayer and an examination of the needs of the people, the preacher is now ready to begin his expository work in the book. The preacher will want to read the book again and again before preaching on it. At present I am concluding preaching the gospel of Mark. I have prayerfully determined I will move next to the book of Galatians. I will read the six chapters of Galatians daily for the next several weeks. I will read, then reread, then read again. G. Campbell Morgan often read a book fifty times before he started his expository work.

Reading the book is important. As you read the book over and over you will begin to get a feel for the content. You will sense the flow of thought the writer presents. The main arguments of the book will begin to emerge. Several years ago, during a week's stay in the hospital, I was able to read Ephesians many times a day. At the end of the week I had a brand new conception of this wonderful book. The truths of Ephesians came alive to me. My heart was afire with the spiritual blessings discussed therein. As you read through a book many times, you will find that you are not only in possession of the book, but that the book is in possession of you.

G. Campbell Morgan gives four rules for the study of a Bible book:

- Read and gain an impression.
- Think and gain an outline.
- Meditate and gain an analysis.
- Sweat and gain an understanding.

My recommendation is that you give a great deal of attention to this matter. The Bible must be read by believers. An unread Bible is like food uneaten, a love letter never read, a buried sword, a road map unstudied, gold never mined.

Richard Moulton, Bible scholar, made this comment, "We have done almost everything that is possible with these Hebrew and Greek writings. We have overlaid them, clause by clause, with exhaustive commentaries; we have translated them, revised the translations, and quarrelled over the revisions . . . There is yet one thing left to do with the Bible: *simply to read it*"(italics added).[4]

Assuming you have read the Bible book enough to get an overall impression of its contents, the time has come to begin the week-by-week work with your preaching paragraph. W. A. Criswell often says, "If you can get a sermon from a verse, preach on a verse; if you can get a sermon from several verses, preach on several verses; if you can get a sermon from a chapter, preach on a chapter." Normally you will find several verses that seem to hang together and give promise of a helpful message for your people. The paragraphs will vary in length according to the flow of ideas in them. Sometimes I preach from three or four verses. At other times, I gather many more. Sometimes I find help in a good reference Bible. The *Scofield Reference Bible* divides the text of Scripture into paragraphs. Also, a Greek New Testament often has the text divided into paragraphs. You may or may not use these paragraph divisions. As you begin to read, let the passage open up to your understanding. Ask yourself, Do I find in these verses a theme that can be preached to my people?

Once you have determined your preaching passage you must again begin to read. The book has already been read as a whole. Now

4. Richard G. Moulton, *A Short Introduction to the Literature of the Bible* (Boston: D.C. Heath, 1901), pp. iii-iv.

you want to read the smaller paragraph. At this point, I read the paragraph over and over. I read; I reread; I read again and again. Often I will read the paragraph ten to twenty times. If the passage is rather complicated I may read even more. I try to do with the paragraph what I did with the entire book. I am seeking an impression of the contents of the selected verses. I am interested in finding out for myself exactly what the verses say. I consider this to be a crucial step in the work of exposition. At this point, I am not so much interested in what others say about the passage. I want firsthand information concerning the meaning of the Scripture.

READ PRAYERFULLY

A passage should be read prayerfully. The Bible is the inspired Word of God. Our reading should be done with the deepest reverence. No man can comprehend the teachings of the Bible in his own ability. He must have the assistance of the Holy Spirit. The same Holy Spirit who inspired men to write the Bible will illuminate our minds, assisting us to understand what we read. Before I read the passage I pray for divine guidance. As I read the passage I am in an atmosphere of expectant prayer. Throughout the whole process of reading the passage prayer plays a prominent role.

READ CAREFULLY

Do not be in a hurry as you read the passage. Take as much time as is necessary. Do not be a tripper. A tripper is one who goes through a country so fast he never sees anything. He doesn't see the beautiful landscape. He never sees the interesting landmarks. He doesn't see the people who live there. He is just passing through, and hurriedly at that. Instead, as you read your Bible, be a traveler. The traveler journeys slowly in order to absorb everything available to his senses. He looks at the magnificent scenery. He observes the interesting sights. He carefully notes the people of the land through which he travels. When it is over he knows where he has been and what he has seen. This is the way the preacher must read his Bible.[5]

Let me make some suggestions about what to look for as you

5. Ibid.

read the passage. Rudyard Kipling says, "I kept six honest serving men; they taught me all I knew; their names are *what* and *why* and *when* and *how* and *where* and *who*. I sent them over land and sea, I sent them east and west; but after they have worked for me I give them all a rest."[6] These six words: *who, what, when, where, how,* and *why* are indispensible study tools. Use them as you read the paragraph.

Ask yourself, Who is the speaker? Who wrote the words I am reading? What kind of person was he? All these matters have probably been dealt with in your beginning reading of the entire book. Keep these matters in mind as you read the preaching paragraph. Also ask, To whom were these words originally addressed? Who are they? What do I know about them? Why was it important for them to read these words? One of the first things you must learn in sermon preparation is to ask questions of your Scripture passage.

Ask yourself about the time the passage was written. What is the importance of the subject matter being written at that particular time? Very often I find a passage actually comes alive when seen in the proper historic setting. Words in 1 John took on an entirely new significance to me when I learned they were written in an atmosphere where gnostics were claiming a special knowledge. John's emphasis upon "know" appeared in a different light altogether.

Be concerned about the place in which the passage was written. Do we know where it was written? Is there any significance to that particular place? For example, we are very interested when we read that Jacob spent the night at Bethel. Bethel means the house of God. The passage has increasing interest when we understand the geographical location.

The occasion that called for the verses to be written is also important. What were the circumstances? Paul's letter to the Galatians becomes more intelligible when we understand that his apostleship was under attack. We are better able to understand the change in his normal introduction when we know that.

Be interested in the purpose of the passage. What is the writer trying to accomplish? What truth is he seeking to convey? What error is he seeking to correct? What encouragement is he trying to give?

See what you can find out about the subject of the passage. Be

6. Ibid., p. 64.

very thorough in your reading. Do not allow what others say about the purpose of the passage to sway you at this point.

Be on the lookout for several other matters. Be aware of any change of persons speaking or being spoken to in the paragraph. Does he change his remarks? Look for any progression in the passage. Does it move through successive stages of argument? Be watching for any naming of examples or instances in the passage. Look within the passage for illustrations of the truth that is being presented.

Sometimes a passage will give a cumulative selection of ideas or teachings. Often, ideas are compared or grouped together in a passage. Look for contrasting ideas in the same passage. Sometimes a passage will give cause-and-effect relationships. Look for repetition of certain clauses. Be aware of transitional statements or phrases. These very often conclude one argument and introduce another. All of these matters will be considered in more detail as we go deeper into the process of exposition. For now, be aware of them in your preliminary reading.

Cloverdale's rules give a neat summary of the kinds of things to look for in your reading: What is spoken? Of whom? With what words? At what time? To what intent?

Meditation upon the passage will yield much fruit. Meditation seems to be a lost art among modern men. Living in a fast-paced society has made meditation increasingly difficult. But the Bible commends the practice. Psalm 1:2 says, "His delight is in the law of the Lord; and in his law doth he meditate day and night." Joshua 1:8 says, "This book of the law shall not depart out of thy mouth; but thou shalt meditate therein day and night, that thou mayest observe to do according to all that is written therein: for then thou shalt make thy way prosperous, and then thou shalt have good success." In the reading of the passage, stop from time to time and put your mind to work on it. Allow your thoughts to travel down many avenues. Suck the verses like a child does an orange. Chew the passage as a cow does its cud. Give time for subconscious incubation. In a later chapter I will discuss the whole matter of time to allow the subconscious mind to work on your sermon. During the reading process, however, take time to meditate all through your reading. As one preacher said, "I sit a long while on my eggs." You will discover that time spent meditating over the passage is not wasted time. Meditation will allow your mind sufficient time to really work into the passage.

READ IMAGINATIVELY

Use your imagination as you read the passage. Imagination is a very helpful tool in getting at the truth of the passage. Imagination can take a familiar truth, bring it to life, and give a new sense of impact and excitement.[7] Put yourself into the passage. Imagine you are actually there. Live out what is taking place in the passage. Role play the people who appear therein. Use your imagination in a responsible manner. Do not go to the extreme. Do allow yourself to live what is being taught. You will be surprised at how much more vivid the passage will become. I find I am helped if I read the passage aloud. I try to imagine the tone of voice and the inflection each speaker has. You will be amazed at the different insights such reading will give you.

Put the passage in contemporary clothing. If you are reading the parable of the prodigal son, bring him into the twentieth century. Visualize him as he gets into his convertible and drives away from his father's house on his way to the big city. Imagine that the prodigal son lives with the family next door. This will help you in understanding the passage better. Be careful you do not distort the meaning of the Scripture by this. Do not be frivolous in your use of imagination. Used in the proper manner, imagination can greatly assist you in your comprehension of what the Scripture paragraph is saying. This is one solution to the problem of getting the meaning of the Scripture passage to your people in a manner they can understand. The difference between a good preacher and an average preacher is right here. Imagination used properly can make a passage come alive. The good preacher is part actor. He learns how to bring Bible characters to life.

READ OBEDIENTLY

After you have read the passage in the manner I have suggested, there is a further step to be taken. The passage should be read obe-

7. Chevis F. Horne, *Dynamic Preaching* (Nashville: Broadman, 1983), p. 52.

diently. As you read the Scripture your own heart and life will be confronted with many truths. The preacher must never confront his people with Bible truths that he himself has failed to face in his own life. The Bible admonishes, "But be ye doers of the word, and not hearers only, deceiving your own selves" (James 1:22). To study the Word of God in order to preach it to others is a deeply searching matter. My own life is weekly rebuked, challenged, and expanded. Be willing to allow your soul to be exposed to the teachings of the Word of God. Accept the responsibility to make any changes in your own life that may be demanded by the Scripture you are preparing to deliver to your people. When you read the Bible in this manner you come to your people not only with a mind saturated in the truths the Word teaches but also with your own heart chastened and cleansed by the imperatives found therein.

LOOK FOR THEME AND MAIN POINTS

In a preliminary way your reading should point you toward a discovery of the unifying theme of the passage. By unifying theme I mean that theme that controls or comprehends the whole thought of the passage. We will discuss further the meaning of the unifying theme later. In your preliminary reading, however, you should be looking for a simple, clear expression of the meaning of the passage. Also, begin to look for certain main divisions. These divisions should point to the unifying theme. Try to express each division in a brief phrase or a word. Many times, after a few readings of the passage, a clear outline emerges. That is always gratifying to the expositor. It points him quickly to the basic structure of his sermon. Unfortunately, the unifying theme and main divisions do not always so readily appear. In many instances the preacher will be quite well into his expository work before he determines the unifying theme and the main divisions. If the preacher can find those during his preliminary reading of the passage, then he is able to spend more time on other aspects of sermon preparation.

SEVERAL CLUES

In seeking to arrive at the meaning of the passage during these beginning readings several clues are useful. Look for repetitions of terms, phrases, clauses, or sentences. As you read 1 Corinthians 13 the word *charity* (love) appears several times. The repetition of the word indicates that *love* is the unifying theme of the chapter. In a study of Amos 1 and 2 a recurring phrase is found: "Thus saith the Lord; For three transgressions of Damascus, and for four, I will not turn away the punishment thereof." This phrase occurs several times. This repetition gives us a clue to the meaning of the passage.

Certain transitional clues often appear as we read. Be aware of these transitional words: then, therefore, wherefore, but, nevertheless, meanwhile. Such transitional words make us sensitive to the introduction of a new thought or to the conclusion of a previous one. When you see the word *therefore*, ask yourself, What is the "therefore" there for? "Therefore" will point us backward or forward. The word *but* is often a corner word in Scripture. You are walking down one road in Scripture, then come to this "corner," and find yourself delightfully upon another road. This is seen in Ephesians 2:1-7. In the first three verses Paul describes the sad condition of the lost person. He is described as one dead in trespasses and sins, walking according to the course of the world, fulfilling the desires of the flesh. In verse 4 we read, "But God!" What a change. Many, many times these transitional clues will be the hinges upon which will turn beautiful interpretations and explanations.

Sometimes our reading will discover the rhetorical question, used effectively. This is vividly seen in Malachi's use of the question, "Wherein?" Be on the lookout for those.

Often a change in time, location, or setting will be a clue to help us understand a passage. This is especially true in the narrative passages in the Bible. Be looking for what details the particular Bible writer has selected and how those details are arranged. Such changes are often found in the four gospels. We are aware that no single gospel writer included all the details in the life of Christ. Why did each writer choose what he did include? What purpose is he seeking to accomplish by the inclusion or exclusion of certain details?

Sometimes the writer himself will give us a clue as to the meaning of the passage. John regularly does this. In John 20:30-31 he tells us why he included the particular miracles given in his gospel. The reader is helped if he will remember John's purpose as he reads each of the miracles recorded. In his first letter, John gives several reasons for its composition. Those should be kept in mind as we interpret 1 John. They give us vital clues to the meaning of his letter. John gives the key to the meaning of the Revelation at the very front of the book (see Rev. 1:19).

All this preliminary reading of the Scripture passage is to be done before you go any further. No reference books have yet been consulted. No word study has been done. You have merely given yourself to a thoughtful reading of the Scripture. You have found for yourself the contents of the Scripture passage. This is a most essential part of sermon preparation. Very often the preacher rushes on to do the technical work and passes over the simple, apparent truths of the passage. Once he has read the Scripture paragraph he is then ready to do a careful analysis of the passage. He moves to that step with a great deal of confidence. He has found out for himself what the passage actually says. He has not depended upon secondary opinions. He himself has read the passage. He knows every turn, shift, and movement in the passage. He knows the material. Now the time has come for him to begin to take the passage apart piece by piece.

Interpretation

The first step in our exposition of the Scripture passage has been taken. We have answered the question, What does the passage say? This gives a significant advantage at this stage in our study. To know the basic ingredients of the passage means we know what the passage says. We have not depended upon what others may say the passage says. We have minutely, carefully, intensely looked at the passage for ourselves. Now the second question must be answered: What does the passage mean? This takes us into the area of interpretation. At this stage, our expository work will become very detailed. Every conceivable method of interpreting the meaning of the passage will be explored. No stone must be left unturned. Our purpose is to find, insofar as possible, the exact meaning of the Scripture passage. We must not be satisfied to say what we think the passage means.

DIAGRAM THE PASSAGE

A block diagram is very useful and illuminating as the work of interpretation is begun. Walter C. Kaiser, Jr., advocates the use of a block diagram. He calls the diagram a "syntactical display." On a sheet of paper the passage is actually diagrammed. The theme proposition, the controlling theme of the passage, is placed on the left margin of the page. Then the syntactical units that directly relate to the theme are slightly indented.[8] I use a somewhat simpler procedure but basically accomplish the same purpose. I try to determine the core of the sentences: that is, the main subject, the main verb, and the main object of each sentence. I do this for each of the sentences in my preaching paragraph. From this I do what is called a textual recreation. In visual form the entire paragraph is laid out. Each sentence is diagrammed. This enables me to readily see the structure of each sentence. Such clues as repetitions, comparisons, and progressions are indented, underlined, or circled and tied together by lines drawn.[9] This enables me to get a picture of the entire passage. Often such a visual recreation of the passage helps me to see the unifying theme and supporting divisions very quickly. This procedure is especially helpful in showing the repetitions that occur. I am better able to tie the passage together when I have seen each section of the passage in relationship to the whole.

Analyzing the manner in which the supporting propositions in a paragraph relate to one another around a single theme is my most difficult assignment. The block diagram, showing the surface of the passage, often supplies many of the clues that lead me toward this single idea. Time spent doing a simple diagram of the passage will pay rich dividends.

DO WORD STUDIES

After I have done a block paragraph I move immediately into word studies. I consider word studies to be most essential in proper exposition. Through careful study of the words and the relationships of the words we can determine the literal meaning of the Bible text. I am interested to know what is the simple, plain, obvious, and literal sense of the words, phrase, clauses, and sentences of the passage.

The older textbooks often refer to the grammatico-historical method of exegesis. The aim of this method was to determine the

8. Kaiser, p. 99.
9. Jensen, p. 77.

meaning of the text by application of the laws of grammar and the available facts of history. "Grammatico" made reference to ascertaining the literal meaning of the text. Kaiser has proposed a new name for the process. He prefers the term *syntactical-theological method of exegesis*. We are primarily interested in the syntactical aspect of exegesis at this point in our study. By syntactical Kaiser means the way the words are put together as well as the meaning of the words themselves as an aid in finding the author's meaning in the passage. Kaiser explains syntactical analysis as operating from three basic building blocks: the concept, the proposition, and the paragraph.

Utilizing my Greek New Testament, or the Hebrew text if I am in the Old Testament, I read through the passage in the original language. I find the meaning of the main words in the passage. Depending upon its length, I may check carefully each word in the passage. If the passage is rather lengthy, I may only look for the meanings of the main words. I have previously recommended to you a knowledge of the original languages. If you do not have the opportunity to study the original languages, do not let this dissuade you. Several good volumes are available to help you in your word study. Those works are mentioned in the section on tools for study.

I have found work in the Greek text especially fruitful. The Greek language abounds in beautiful word pictures. A veritable treasure house of preaching material may be found in the meanings of the Greek words. From the original languages get the meanings of the words. Know the definition of each term in the passage and exactly how the term is used. Find the root meaning of the word. What preaching suggestions do you find there? The preacher must be aware of special idioms and rare words in Scripture selection.

Keep in mind several factors as you do your word study. Find the usage of a word at the time of the author. The author's definition of the word is most advantageous. Many times this can be discovered by a quick reference to other passages where the author uses the same word. Determine the grammatical use of the word. See if a particular word is used in contrast with other words in your passage. The contrast between "flesh" and "Spirit" in Romans 8:5-8 gives you a fruitful preaching passage. Look for the meaning of the words of your passage in parallel passages. Let me caution you that words are used with different meanings in different books of the Bible. Each author may have a particular way in which he uses a word. That peculiarity may not be uniform in another passage. Further, be aware of the cultural use of terms. Attention to background studies later on in the chapter will demonstrate the importance of cultural terms in the Scriptures.

When I am doing this particular part of my exposition, to some degree I try to examine each word or phrase. I seek to determine as accurately as I can the meaning of the words. To adequately interpret the meaning of the passage one must know the meaning of the words in their original usage. Sometimes the original meaning of a word is absolutely essential to the interpretation of the passage.[10]

Every language has particular modes of expression and methods of phrasing that are peculiar to that language. These forms of speech are part and parcel of the particular language. We must know these idioms. Their knowledge can change the meaning of a passage. Unger cites an example from Genesis 2:17. In that verse we read, "Thou shalt surely die." Literally translated the phrase means, "a dying thou shall die." This is an idiom peculiar to the Hebrew language. Knowing this affects our understanding of this Scripture.[11]

Never minimize the use of a particular word. Jensen says, "Just as a great door swings on small hinges, the important theological statements of the Bible often depend upon even the smallest words, such as prepositions and articles. Using another picture, one writer has said that as the smallest dewdrop on the meadow at night has a star sleeping in its bosom, so the most insignificant passage of Scripture has in it a shining truth."[12]

I have found several guidelines helpful in weighing the meaning of a word. I always check occurrences in the Bible. This can be done with a good exhaustive concordance. I have previously mentioned finding the root meaning of a word. This is done by consulting your Hebrew or Greek lexicon. Sometimes insight is gained by finding a word's usage in extrabiblical literature. *The Vocabulary of the Greek New Testament,* by James H. Moulton and George Milligan, is a very good resource for this. I try to find the most frequent usage of a word in the Bible. Also, I compare the Old and New Testament usage of the word.

10. Unger, p. 120.
11. Ibid., p. 122.
12. Jensen, p. 96.

As you do word study you must be aware of the presence of figures of speech in the Bible. Language would be very dull and drab without figures of speech. They add warmth, color, and life to a language. My first approach to understanding a Scripture passage is to take the words in their literal meaning. I agree with Unger's statement: "When the plain sense of Scripture makes common sense, seek no other sense; therefore, take every word at its primary, usual, literal meaning, unless it is patently a rhetorical figure or unless the immediate context, studied carefully in the light of related passages and axiomatic and fundamental truths, clearly points otherwise."[13]

Sometimes the words cannot be taken in their literal meanings. There are times when the literal proves to be absurd, would make them inconsistent with the other parts of the sentence, or would do violence to the nature of the subject discussed. When this occurs, we are to understand that the language is figurative. You might ask yourself the following questions: If I take the meaning to be literal, will this be consistent with the general content of the passage? Does a literal meaning coincide with the historical material or the doctrinal subject found in the passage? This will help you to avoid some absurd interpretations.

Many figures of speech occur in the Bible. Simile, an imaginative comparison, is a rhetorical device in which two things are compared to each other. Certain words in the passage tip us off to the use of simile. Words such as *like, as,* or *so* indicate the use of simile.[14] The teaching of Jesus abounds in simile. Jesus said, "The kingdom of heaven is likened unto a man which sowed good seed in his field" (Matt. 13:24); again, it is "like unto leaven" hid in meal (Matt. 13:33).

Metaphor is commonly used in the Bible. A metaphor is an implied likeness in which words such as *like, as,* or *so* are omitted. Jesus used metaphor. He said, "Ye are the salt of the earth" (Matt. 5:13); "Ye are the light of the world" (Matt. 5:14).

There are times when the language of paradox is used. A paradoxical statement is one that seems so absurd or contrary to general opinion that it immediately catches attention in order to emphasize truth. Jesus used paradox often to teach truth. He said to His disciples,

13. Unger, p. 176.
14. Ibid., p. 178.

"For whosoever will save his life shall lose it: and whosoever will lose his life for my sake shall find it" (Matt. 16:25).

Hyperbole is sometimes used in Scripture. Hyperbole is the use of exaggeration in order to emphasize some truth. Jesus said, talking about the impossibility of going to heaven by means of riches, "It is easier for a camel to go through the eye of a needle, than for a rich man to enter into the kingdom of God" (Matt. 19:24).

As you interpret the meaning of a passage you must constantly be aware of these figures of speech. They can change your understanding of the teaching of the passage.

To summarize, do thorough word study. Find out the literal meaning of the words. Be aware of the possibility of the words being used in a particular way by the author for a special purpose. Be cognizant that sometimes figures of speech are used in the Bible. That in no way takes away from the literal meaning of the passage that is being conveyed. Rather, such devices of language add to the meaning the full richness of the inspired words and their usage.

After you have done a thorough word study, give attention to grammar. Words do not occur in isolation. They occur in relation to one another. The verbs have certain tenses. Are the verbs in the present tense, past tense, future tense? Be sensitive to the relation of the words to one another. If you are not able to fully understand the syntactical relationships of the passage, check a good word study volume. A. T. Robertson's *Word Pictures in the New Testament* is very helpful in this regard. The way the words are put together indicate the author's meaning. Do not overlook this area of word study.

When you have completed a word study of the passage you will have in hand a great deal of material. Not all the material you have gathered will be used. Avoid taking all of the technical baggage to the pulpit. As some wag said about her scholarly pastor, "If he doesn't Hebrew-root you to death, he will strangle you to death with Greek participles!" The people to whom you preach will most likely not be interested in the technical details of your study. This does not mean you will not do technical exegesis. Do all the spade work, then glean the preaching riches for your sermon. Leave the nuts and bolts in your study.

The richest area of my sermonic preparation for many years has been word study. A study of the words has become a source of endless sermon material for me. My own heart has been blessed with firsthand knowledge of the meaning of the text. Those who have listened to me preach have also profited. A careful word study of your passage will be worth the effort.

STUDY THE CONTEXT

A key ingredient in determining the meaning of a passage of Scripture is what Kaiser calls contextual analysis. Exposition demands that we be familiar with the immediate context. Determine how the passage fits in with the overall context of the book in which it is found. Further, look at the passage of Scripture in light of the total revelation and message of the Bible. This is an essential part of my expository work. I do not know who made the statement, but I agree: "Text without context is pretext." Many doctrinal errors occur because the context of a Scripture passage is often ignored or misunderstood.

The word *context* comes from two Latin words: *con*, which means "with" or "together", and *texere*, which means " to weave." The context has to do with something woven together. For the purpose of our study, context is defined as that part of a discourse in which the passage occurs. The context guides us in explaining the meaning of the passage.[15] The part must be seen in relationship to the whole.

In an organism, no member or part, however minute, can be adequately explained apart from its relation to the whole; even so, every paragraph of Scripture has a connection with its totality. Each paragraph of Scripture must be studied in relation to all the rest. Our preaching paragraph will be illuminated by the context. The Scripture verses immediately preceding and following the passage must be carefully considered. Never lift a paragraph (or individual verses) from its contextual setting. A paragraph must be studied in relation to the connection of thought that runs through an entire section.

Because of the importance of contextual study it is necessary for the expository preacher to have a working knowledge of the various books of the Bible. Robinson says, "What a writer means in any specific paragraph or chapter can be determined basically by fitting

15. Ibid., p. 142.

it into the larger argument of the book. This is the broad context."[16] Several books are helpful in giving us an overview of each book of the Bible. John Phillips's *Exploring the Scriptures* is a good, one-volume survey of the books of the Bible. He gives a brief, pertinent introduction to each book as well as a helpful outline and a few brief paragraphs summarizing the contents of each book. A large, more extensive work is J. Sidlow Baxter's four-volume *Explore the Book.* Dr. Baxter gives very helpful introductory material on each book of the Bible. Valuable insights and clues that aid in understanding each Bible book make Dr. Baxter's work indispensable. Do not attempt to expound a book of the Bible without first understanding the basic truths and emphases that are made. Know the plan of each Bible writer in putting his book together. When you understand the author's plan and his approach, many otherwise obscure details will become clear and understandable.

Let us go a step further. To be aware of a book's location in the canon is often crucial. The Bible is divided into certain kinds of literature. The first seventeen books of the Bible (Genesis through 2 Chronicles) are historical in nature. The next five books (Job through Song of Solomon) are poetical in their literary form. The last seventeen books of the Old Testament are books of prophecy (Isaiah through Malachi). In the new Testament, the first five books (Matthew through Acts) are historical. The next twenty-one are letters (Romans through Jude). The last book of the New Testament (Revelation) is apocalyptic literature. When you are studying in a particular book of the Bible know its literary form.

As Kaiser has pointed out there are five basic literary forms in the Bible. *Prose* is the normal, daily speech of mankind. Much descriptive prose is found in the Bible. Also included are expository prose, polemical prose, historical narratives, and so on. When you are reading prose an awareness of this will aid you.

Kaiser lists poetry second. One third of the Old Testament is poetry. An understanding of the method of Hebrew poetry will affect your interpretation of a Scripture passage. Old Testament poetry does not rhyme. Rather, there is a parallelism of ideas.

Third, Kaiser lists historical narrative. This is present in the four

16. Haddon W. Robinson, *Biblical Preaching* (Grand Rapids: Baker, 1980), p. 58.

gospels and in the book of Acts. We must keep in mind when we read from these sections that we are reading historical narratives. Kaiser cautions that we must be careful to bridge the gap from the "then" to the "now." This will have much to do in making our preaching more contemporary.

Kaiser lists the wisdom writings fourth. Much of this literature is reflective and philosophical in nature. Such a book as Ecclesiastes falls into this category.

Fifth, Kaiser mentions apocalyptic literature. This kind of literature is rich in symbolism. We are specifically told that the book of Revelation is written in this manner. In Revelation 1:1 John says God gave the message of the Revelation in sign form. "He sent and signified it by his angel unto his servant, John." This immediately gives us the clue that much of the truth of Revelation is given in sign form. The preacher who wants to be as correct as possible in his interpretation of Scripture will not fail to take into consideration the kind of literature with which he is dealing.[17]

I am also convinced that the passage of Scripture you are studying must be studied in relation to the whole revelation of the Bible. Donald Grey Barnhouse illustrates this by means of an inverted pyramid. He says the particular passage you are studying is like the point on a straight line. The entire revelation of the Bible is like an inverted pyramid. This inverted pyramid is brought to bear upon that single point. He means that we must study our passage of Scripture in relation to the whole teaching of the Bible. If your interpretation of a particular passage contradicts the clear teaching of the whole Bible, you can assume you are astray in your interpretation.

I have found this understanding very helpful in explaining the meaning of some obscure passages in the Bible. What is obscure must be interpreted by what is clear. That which is briefly mentioned must be interpreted by that which is is distinctly, clearly, abundantly expressed throughout the Word of God. Never allow yourself to be robbed of the value of what you do understand by something which you do not understand. The one is founded upon knowledge; the other is based upon ignorance.

Give close attention to the immediate connection of your passage

17. Kaiser, pp. 91-93.

with the context. Kaiser says there are various types of those connections. First, there is the historical. Look for connections of events or facts in the passage. Second is the theological connection. Some doctrine may be stated in this particular section. Your preaching paragraph may be an integral part of this theological argument. Third, the logical connection. The author may be building a particular line of truth. The paragraph under your consideration may be a part of this development. Fourth, the psychological connection. Something stated in the verses prior to the paragraph under consideration may have led the author to the particular thought now being expressed in your preaching paragraph. Sometimes you will find a passage seems to be totally unrelated to what has previously been said. Careful examination, however, will reveal that the idea is related in some way.[18]

GATHER THE HISTORICAL DATA

Previously I mentioned that Kaiser refers to the grammatico-historical method of exegesis. We have taken some space to discuss the importance of word study and also contextual study. Now we turn our attention to background or historical study, the time and circumstances in which the author wrote. Kaiser points up a common problem in expository sermonizing at this juncture. He believes that too much exegesis has failed to "map the route between the actual determination of the authentic meaning and the delivery of that word to modern men and women who ask that that meaning be translated into some kind of normative application or significance for their lives."[19] This caution should be carefully considered. We will attempt to bridge the gap between our exegetical studies and the preparation of a message that will be helpful and practical to our listeners. But let us not minimize the importance of doing adequate and thorough background study. The historical setting, the customs of the times, the political and religious conditions are all involved in an adequate interpretation of a passage of Scripture. Very often the political and religious conditions learned through background studies will make a passage much more understandable. In Judges 21:25 we are told, "In those days

18. Ibid., p. 84.
19. Ibid., p. 88.

there was no king in Israel: every man did that which was right in his own eyes." This statement illuminates all of the material in the book of Judges.

Certain phrases and sentences will be made more understandable through background study. Some figures of speech will be hard to understand apart from the particular historical setting in which they are found.

Gathering the background data will involve several matters. Who wrote the passage under our consideration? Who was he? Understanding the human author will sometimes help us get to the meaning of a passage better. To know the particular interest of the author in writing is always important.

We must also seek to ascertain the speaker in a Scripture passage. Is the speaker different from the writer? Why is he speaking at this particular time? Is he answering a question?

To know those who first read the passage will be a pertinent piece of data. Why were these words addressed to them? What would their response be? This will very often make a passage come alive to you. Such matters as the time the passage was written, the place where written, and the occasion of writing all are discovered through background studies. Be sure to look up every mention of a place or occasion. A good Bible dictionary will provide good background material on the various locations in the Bible lands. Discover all you can about these places.

Certain times of the year give insight into the meaning of a Scripture passage. If this Scripture passage occurred during the Passover, for instance, what is the significance to be derived from that? You must have some understanding of the Passover to answer this question. Be as thorough as you can in these matters.

To know the stage of revelation of the particular passage you are studying affects proper interpretation. This is important because there is a progressive unfolding of God's truth throughout the Bible. Failure to recognize this is the cause of many tragic misinterpretations. Bible doctrine is not built on Old Testament revelation alone. We must have the entire revelation of God on a subject as we interpret Scripture. Because this is true we must be keenly aware of the stage of revelation in which our particular Scripture passage is found.

Do as much background study as you possibly can. Make note

of every historical detail that may be contained in the Scripture passage under consideration. All these details will combine to give you a better basis for understanding the passage.

DO CROSS-REFERENCE WORK

One of the best methods of interpreting Scripture is to allow Scripture to interpret Scripture. I call this cross-reference work. Know what other passages of Scripture have to say about the subjects discussed in the passage you are examining. This really carries the concept of contextual analysis to its practical application. Draw from the entire Word of God what is said about any particular subject.

If the theme of your Scripture passage is grace, find out what other parallel passages have to say about grace. Check the word *grace* in your Bible concordance. Read all the references on grace. Allow Scripture to interpret Scripture. A learned Bible scholar gave a copy of his commentary on Matthew to his gardener. A few days later the scholar asked his gardener, "What do you think about my commentary on Matthew?" His Bible-taught gardener replied, "Doctor, the Bible sure does throw a lot of light on your commentary!" This statement is true as well as humorous.

Several years ago I ran across a very helpful book in cross-reference work, *The Treasury of Scripture Knowledge*. This book, published by the Fleming H. Revell Company, lists 500,000 Scripture references and parallel passages. I have been blessed by use of the parallel passages found in this book. This reference work has often given to me just the added light and insight I needed. There are few passages in the Bible that cannot be explained and made much clearer by other passages.

Cross reference work is a very valuable aid to correct interpretation. Spend some time in your sermonic preparation doing parallel studies. You will find your understanding of Scripture is greatly strengthened.

DETERMINE THE THEOLOGICAL SIGNIFICANCE

We have not completed our work of interpretation until we have studied the theological significance of the passage. This is mandatory to good exposition. The Bible is a book of theology. The theology of the Bible is a unity. The Old Testament and the New Testament agree on theological truths. Though there is a progressive unfolding of the theological truths found in the Bible, there is great unity throughout. The great theme of redemption runs all the way through the Bible. One might say that the entire Bible is an unfolding of the simple message of John 3:16. All the way through the Scriptures we read of God's great love for man, His grief at man's sin, and His determination to send a Savior to make possible man's redemption from sin. The Old Testament in its history, typology, and prophetical pronouncements is a preparation for the coming of the Lord Jesus Christ. The Old Testament could be summarized in one brief statement: He is coming! For this reason the Old Testament cannot be separated from the New Testament.

Likewise, the New Testament must always be studied in light of the Old Testament. The New Testament provides us with a commentary on the Old. We must always give attention to the teachings of the New Testament as we search for correct interpretation of the Old.

Kaiser's *Towards an Exegetical Theology* makes a significant contribution to the study of Bible exposition, particularly in this area. Dr. Kaiser contends that failure on the part of the exegete to adequately determine the theological interpretation of the passage is the reason for much irrelevant and dull Bible exposition. Kaiser maintains that there is always in a passage of Scripture a theological content that has its roots antecedent to the passage. He maintains that a thorough examination of biblical theology is essential to accurate interpretation. Kaiser explains that the good exegete should keep on hand a volume on biblical theology. Further, he recommends that the use of the words of a passage be found. At the end of his chapter on theological analysis he provides a good bibliography of helpful works on theological analysis.[20] Consult this bibliography for several volumes you might like to purchase.

Studying the theological significance of your passage of Scripture will bring you in contact with truths of the passage that can be related in a practical way to your people. Again, Kaiser points out that many pastors only give a historical recounting of what took place in the Bible world. Too often this is not related in any practical way to the

20. Ibid., p. 147.

real world of those who listen. For this reason, expository preaching is considered by some to be dull and uninteresting. Kaiser compares this kind of preaching to a ball carrier carrying the football to within twenty-five yards of the end zone and then asking God's people to carry it the rest of the way.[21]

Preachers make many attempts to avoid this problem. They get involved in spiritualizing a passage, giving a "Bible editorial" on some selected passage of Scripture, or looking for a few moral lessons that can be drawn from the verses. All of these inadequate attempts to derive practical lessons from the Scriptures can be avoided. Look for the timeless truths in the Scripture passage you are studying. As you interpret the passage, ask yourself, What is God doing? Be aware that the Bible is not given primarily to be a historical study. The purpose of any Scripture passage is to bring timeless truth to real people in a real world.

Finding the theological truths in a passage can help you relate in a practical way to your congregation. Horne says, "It is not enough to do an accurate exegetical study of the text and then enter the historical situation imaginatively. Another step has to be taken: the truth has to be transposed so it can speak to the needs and demands of today's life."[22] This can be done through discovering the theological significance of a passage of Scripture. Truth is truth whenever and wherever found. The great theological truths that spoke to the hearts of the Bible people can speak to our own day as well. Spend much time in your work of interpretation in this area.

CONSULT COMMENTARIES

I mention the use of commentaries last because commentary study must not be allowed to unduly sway one in the matter of interpretation. We are interested to discover for ourselves what the passage actually says. In order to determine this for ourselves we need to go into the matters which I have already discussed in this chapter. There is the temptation to prematurely check to see what a commentary says about a passage of Scripture. Avoid that temptation. Rigorously discipline your study to linger over the Bible passage itself until you have

21. Ibid., p. 132.
22. Horne, p. 174.

deciphered the truths and meanings for yourself. I do not disparage the use of outside helps. I merely urge that you not allow them to become crutches upon which you lean. Commentaries are intended to be tools to aid you in your study. They are never intended to be information received as final authority. Do the hard work for yourself. After you have made every attempt to discover the meaning of the passage on your own, then you will be ready to see what others have said about the same passage.

What others have written on a Scripture passage serve as checkpoints for my own interpretation. If my interpretation leads me far afield from good, solid expositors, I need to look very carefully at my interpretation. I do not mean by this that you will not from time to time differ with most or all of your commentaries. But, if you come to an interpretation of the passage that is diametrically opposed to the consensus of solid Bible commentaries, you could be wrong.

Very often commentaries will shed additional light on your passage. God does not give all truth to any man. God's truth is the property of His church. Look for helpful insights on your Scripture passage from many sources. We will not lift a man's expressions of thought and merely place them in our message. We will take his insights into the fertile soil of our own mind, allow them to become part of us, and then express them in a way that is consistent with our own understanding and methods of expression. All truth God gives to men can be used in preaching truth to others. Commentaries help us think through the truths we confront in Scripture. They trigger our thinking. When used in this manner they can be very helpful to us.

Let me also give you a word of warning. One may become enamored with a particular Bible commentator. His writing may so closely coincide with your own thinking that you find yourself constantly referring to his work. Do not allow yourself to become a slave to any man. The best of Bible expositors may go astray in their interpretations from time to time. Don't sell your soul to any of them. Learn to bring every commentary to the judgment of Scripture. If you are benefited by the writings of a particular man, fine. Just do not regard his writings as the final word on the Scriptures.

From time to time I find my own thought processes stimulated by reading men with whom I strongly disagree. This confirms me in my own conviction about the interpretation I have found for myself. Do not restrict yourself to reading only those who agree with you. Very often some of my best insights have come as a result of reading men with whom I disagree.

I have found little value in commentaries on the whole Bible. I have several of them on the shelves of my study. I hardly, if ever, consult them. The reason is very simple: What little good I have ever gleaned from them has been hardly worth the time and effort involved in reading through these commentaries. I am a busy pastor. My time is at a premium. I cannot spend large blocks of my time reading through material that has very little usable information for my preaching ministry.

This has led me to a different method of commentary study. Rather than consulting whole Bible commentaries, I have tried to find the best individual commentaries on the book which I am currently expounding. After a few weeks of preaching through a particular book I find which of the commentaries are the richest and most valuable. Some of the books I lay aside. I concentrate on those that have the best material.

APPLY PROPER PRINCIPLES OF INTERPRETATION

I want to conclude this section with a brief discussion of some principles of Bible interpretation that are valuable in correct interpretation. What I am giving here is certainly not exhaustive. I mention just a few principles of interpretation. A good volume on Bible hermeneutics will give you a fuller explanation of the basic laws of Bible interpretation. Paul says in 2 Timothy 2:15 that we are to rightly divide the Word of truth. The phrase *rightly dividing* actually means "cutting straight." The phrase was used in classical Greek of a surgeon's cutting or using a knife. The least deviation meant death to the patient.[23] We are dealing with issues of life and death to those who listen to us preach. We must understand and use the principles of correct interpretation. If laws of interpretation are violated, we go astray in adequately expounding what the passage actually means.

The *ethnic division* principle is important. In 1 Corinthians 10:32,

23. Unger, pp. 164-65.

the entire human race is divided into three categories: the Jew, the Gentile, and the church. All Scripture is addressed to one of these three categories. Always ask when reading a passage: To whom was this written? This will affect your interpretation. Much misinterpretation of Scripture is due to a confusing of those passages written specifically to the Jew and those written to the church. Although all Scripture applies to us, not all is necessarily addressed to us. Keeping the ethnic division principle in mind will help you avoid misapplying many of the Old Testament prophecies that are addressed to the nation Israel. Literal promises were given to the Jewish people. They will be literally fulfilled. As Romans 15:4 suggests, those things written in the Old Testament are helpful for our learning and in bringing patience and comfort to our lives. But we must not appropriate promises that were specifically given to the Jewish nation.

The *first mention* principle will sometimes give you a clue to the meaning of a passage. The first time a subject is mentioned is very often the key to its meaning. In Genesis 3:1 the Bible mentions Satan for the first time. We are told that Satan is very "subtle." This sets the tone for scriptural information on Satan throughout the Bible. The first mention principle makes the book of Genesis very important in matters of interpretation. This is why some have referred to Genesis as the seed plot of the Bible.

Another important principle is the *full mention* principle. Very often subjects in the Bible are given one comprehensive treatment somewhere in the Bible. For instance, faith is given a full treatment in Hebrews 11. An understanding of faith can be gained from a careful study of this chapter. Love is mentioned quite comprehensively in 1 Corinthians 13. Sometimes God declares His full revelation on a particular subject in one place in the Bible.

There is also the principle of *proportionate mention*. The amount of space given in Scripture to a particular theme needs to be noted. Truth out of proportion can become error. We must be sure that we magnify those truths that Scripture magnifies. We must not dwell upon truths that are mentioned only briefly in Scripture. Many false doctrines result from failing to maintain the balance the Bible does.

The principle of *repeated mention* is important. Very often the Holy Spirit will first give only the bare outline of a subject. Then, as the subject is repeated again and again, added details will be included. One will be fascinated to see how the recurrence of certain truths adds new information throughout the total revelation of the Bible. Many, many doctrines open up throughout the passages of Scripture as a beautiful flower.

An understanding of the *gap* principle can shed light upon the meaning of a passage. On occasion God ignores certain periods of time, leaping over many centuries without comment. This is seen in Isaiah 61:1-2. These verses obviously are messianic in nature. They give a beautiful picture of the characteristics of the ministry of our Lord. In verse 2 Isaiah says the Messiah would come "to proclaim the acceptable year of the Lord, and the day of vengeance of our God." Between the phrases "to proclaim the acceptable year of the Lord" and "the day of vengeance of our God" many centuries have passed. Jesus makes this obvious by His use of the prophecy in Luke 4:17-20. In the synagogue in Nazareth He read the verses from Isaiah 61:1-2. When He came to the phrase "to preach the acceptable year of the Lord," He closed the book and said, "This day is this Scripture fulfilled in your ears" (Luke 4:21). By so doing Jesus clearly indicated that His first coming fulfilled only the first part of the prophecy. The second part of the prophecy will be fulfilled when He comes again. The gap principle can be cited in several passages of Scripture. Look for such gaps. Your interpretation of Scripture will be invaluably aided.

Another principle that has meant a great deal to me in my expository work is the *salvation/fellowship* principle. Very often one is helped to know whether a passage is a salvation passage or a fellowship passage. Scripture distinguishes between being in God's family and God's fellowship. If a passage of Scripture deals with salvation, we understand the verses in one way. However, if the verses have to do with the matter of fellowship, we understand them in another way. This principle is important in accurately interpreting such passages as John 15. Is this a salvation or a fellowship passage? If we are dealing with a salvation passage, then the verses teach that a person can lose his salvation. This most surely contradicts one of the greatest, most fundamental truths in the entire Scriptures. Obviously, then, the passage is about the matter of fellowship. Jesus is not talking about the loss of salvation. Rather, He is talking about maintaining fellowship with Jesus Christ, which is essential to bearing fruit. Failure to bear fruit results in loss of reward. This particular principle has been invaluable to me in matters of interpretation.

The *threefold* principle is also a helpful principle in interpretation. God's great truth of salvation is presented in a threefold way. One can be biblically correct in saying, "I have been saved; I am being saved; I will be saved." Salvation is presented in these three ways in the Scriptures. *Justification* presents the past aspect of our salvation; *sanctification* presents the present process of our salvation; *glorification* sets forth the future dimension of our salvation.

The *recurrence* principle will serve you well as you interpret certain sections of Scripture. God's Word may state a subject again from a different viewpoint, with a different purpose. Failure to understand this principle of interpretation has caused some to miss what is intended in Genesis 1 and 2. There is really no contradiction between the two chapters. In Genesis 1 the Holy Spirit sets forth creation from a chronological point of view. The emphasis is upon God's creative power. The name for God emphasizing His majesty and His might is used. In the Genesis 2 account the same subject, creation, is presented, but from a different viewpoint. The emphasis in Genesis 2 is not upon chronology. The account is thematic in nature. God's grandest creative work, the creation of man, is given the prominent place. The name for God that emphasizes God's covenant relation to man is used. There is no contradiction. This is merely an instance of the recurrence principle.

We have gone into much detail on the matter of interpretation. Our purpose is to answer the question, What does the Scripture passage mean? We have not wasted our time. Unless we find out what the passage means, we are not ready to move to the third step: How does the passage apply to my life and to the lives of those who will listen to the sermon? The bulk of your study time will be spent right here. Exposition is the main business of the expositor. What we are doing is digging out of the Word itself what is actually said—and what is meant by what is said. This is not the end of our work. To stop here is to have only the bones of exposition. Only the nuts and bolts of our sermon are in our hands. We must press on to the next step in the process.

Application

A great deal of concern is expressed today about the lack of moral convictions on the part of the average churchgoer. A George Gallup poll taken in the spring of 1984 revealed that more people were going to church than ever before, but there was no corresponding lifting of moral standards in American society. Many have expressed concern about the lack of moral change on the part of the average church member. Somewhere along the way multitudes of those who regularly attend church services have failed to make the connection between the truths of the Bible and their moral implications for daily life. I am not seeking to oversimplify the problem. There are perhaps many reasons for this lack of moral awareness on the part of modern churchgoing Americans. One factor that may contribute to the problem is the failure to apply Bible truth to the daily lives of those who listen to sermons.

This is why the third and final step in the work of the Bible expositor is so important. We have taken the first step: investigation. We have answered to our satisfaction the question, What does the passage say? Next, we have taken the second step: interpretation, answering the question, What does the passage mean? We are now ready to take step three: application, What does the passage tell me, and the people to whom I preach, to do?

SELF-APPLICATION

This becomes a deeply soul-searching experience for the preacher. Week by week as I prepare expository sermons I am personally confronted with God's truth, which I have found in the passage of Scripture I am studying. I must face God's truth in my own heart and life. I must never deal in unfelt truth. I cannot preach to others what has not been first of all preached to myself. To do so is to face the danger Paul expressed in 1 Corinthians 9:27, "Lest that by any means, when I have preached to others, I myself should be a castaway." All through the week as I dig into my Scripture passage my study becomes a meeting place with God. Very often I find my heart rebuked by the truths that become increasingly apparent to me throughout my study. I am driven to honestly face the ramifications of the truths I uncover. When I have applied the truths of God's Word to my own life I am then better able to apply them to the lives of my people.

APPLICATION TO THE PEOPLE

Bible truth must be brought to bear in a practical way upon the lives of our people. As I have already indicated, much of the ineffective expository preaching of our day is due to the failure to relate Bible facts to the contemporary world. The preacher must not be content simply to find out the meaning of a few Bible facts. What do these facts mean today? After you have done everything you can to expound the meaning of the passage, ask yourself the question: So what? What does this have to say to my people? When you organize the message later you will want to be sure that definite application is made all along the way. Make the applications from each section of the passage as you go along. D. Martyn Lloyd-Jones says, "It is important that you should have been applying what you have been saying as you go along. There are many ways of doing this. You can do so by asking questions and answering them or in various other ways; but you must apply the message as you go along."[24]

In your thinking you must quickly move from "they" to "you." Move from what the passage meant to what it means. Spurgeon says where the application begins, there the sermon begins; we are not to speak before the people but to them. We must earnestly strive to make them take to themselves what we say. John Broadus quotes Daniel Webster, "When a man preaches to me, I want him to make it a personal matter, a personal matter, a personal matter!"[25]

To fail to make practical application of the Word of God is to do injustice to the Bible's purpose. God's truth is timeless. God was thinking of us when He wrote the Bible. The Word of God is alive. Scripture is as current and up-to-date today as in the days when Bible writers first wrote. The Bible spoke in its time to real people, in real places, who had real problems. The basic problems of life have not

24. D. Martyn Lloyd-Jones, *Preaching and Preachers* (Grand Rapids: Zondervan, 1971), p. 77.
25. John A. Broadus, *The Preparation and Delivery of Sermons* (New York: Harper, 1926), p. 210.

changed. The labels may have changed, but the problems are basically the same. Ask yourself, What timeless truths in this passage of Scripture can I relate to the daily lives of my people? What does this passage have to say about their home lives? Can my young people apply these truths to difficulties they encounter at school? How? I have businessmen sitting in my congregation. What will this truth mean to them at the board meeting in the morning? Will my message give them any guidance concerning the business proposition they will be facing tomorrow? Some of the people in my congregation are facing sickness. Is there something from God's Word that can give them relief and comfort in their suffering? Dig into the Word and draw therefrom practical truths that can touch your people where they hurt.

The subject of application in the work of exposition has not received sufficient attention. In many of the older texts on sermon preparation there is very little helpful guidance concerning how to apply the truth of Scripture to contemporary life. In more recent works the subject has been given more consideration. This is a helpful trend in expository literature. Much more work needs to be done. In many ways application is the most important step in our expository work. All we have done to this point has very little practical value if we cannot make concrete applications.

We must ask ourselves, What is the significance of the meaning we have discovered? We must link what we have found in the Scriptures to life situations, circumstances encountered by our people, and needs that cry out for solutions in their daily existence. Every interpretation we draw from Scripture must have application to the current problems of people.

GUIDELINES TO APPLICATION

The Bible expositor must keep in mind that the Bible is a book written for real people. As Kaiser has suggested, the words of Scripture are directed to specific people who are in specific situations at specific times and in specific cultures.[26] The Bible was not written by a series of authors who were divorced from life. The writers of Scripture were living life alongside the people who would be reading

26. Kaiser, p. 37.

what they wrote. They themselves drew strength from the living Word of God.

Horne points out two questions that were asked by God after sin entered Eden, bringing shame and misery. The first question was directed to man: "Where art thou?" (Gen. 3:9). The second was asked about man: "Where is Abel, thy brother?" (Gen. 4:9).[27] The Bible is interested in man's relationship to God and in man's relationship to man. All through the Bible these themes are constantly repeated. The Bible asks: What is your relation to God? What is your relation to your brother? These questions are just as pertinent today as they were at the time of Adam and Eve. This is only one example of the timely issues that are confronted by the Scriptures.

As you do your expository work ask yourself, What is the human condition to which the timely truths of this passage may be addressed? To keep this in mind is to gear one's thinking to the need for practical application in your completed sermon. I am constantly looking for practical application at every stage of my expository work.

Kaiser says that we must ask, "What are the contemporary equivalents of this shared human condition?"[28] I have found it very helpful to visualize certain members of my congregation as I study through a Scripture passage. I am constantly asking myself, What does this passage have to say to John Smith? Or Pam Jones? Or Billy Foster? Horne mentions a helpful practice followed by Alexander Maclaren. As Maclaren studied the Scriptures during his sermon preparation he placed across from his desk an empty chair. He imagined a person sitting in the chair as he prepared his sermons. He carried on a dialogue between himself and the imaginary person.[29] Such a practice would be helpful in keeping us aware at all times that we are preparing our message for real people.

THE TIMELESS TRUTHS

Kaiser also has an interesting concept in the matter of Scripture application that he calls "principlization." In *Toward an Exegetical Theology* (chap. 7), he discusses this concept. By "principlization"

Kaiser means: When you find the essence and main points of a Scripture passage, state this meaning in the *timeless truths* that apply to the current needs of your people.[30] As he reminds us, the Scriptures handle the major problems of life: Who am I? Why am I here? Where am I going? How may I get rid of guilt? What about love? Marriage? Relationship with others? Death and eternity? The expositor will answer these questions from the truths he finds in his Scripture passage. As he moves through the passage he will draw from its verses rebukes, challenges, appeals, and encouragements. When he puts together the introduction of his message he will seek to arouse interest in his hearers by indicating some of the human needs that will be dealt with in the message. As the expositor moves through the main points of his sermon, he will state them in such a way as to apply to the needs he has mentioned in his introduction. As the expository preacher puts together his conclusion, he will gather all the practical ingredients of the Scripture passage from which he preaches. He will apply Scripture definitely and directly to his hearers in one final, stirring appeal to their hearts.

A REAL BOOK PREACHED BY A REAL PERSON

The expository preacher can make practical application to his people because the Bible is a real book preached by a real person. As I have already indicated in this chapter, the preacher has faced the truths of the Bible in his own life. He has applied them to himself. The message of the Word of God does not come to the listener apart from a living personality. The preacher will "flesh out" the truth of Scripture as he delivers the message. Preaching that is best able to apply powerfully to the listeners is incarnational in nature. The living Word of God is communicated through human flesh. Nothing is so powerfully applicable as the message of salvation communicated through the life of a redeemed man.

FROM THE BIBLE WORLD TO TODAY'S WORLD

Application of scriptural truth can best be made when the preacher knows as much as possible about contemporary man. The preacher's

30. Kaiser, p. 152.

knowledge of man as he lives life today makes possible a positive flow between the Bible world and the modern world. This enables him to preach the eternal Word in such a way that his people get the message.

John R. W. Stott, in his book *Between Two Worlds,* makes some very helpful suggestions concerning how to apply the truths of God's Word to modern congregations. He correctly affirms that application is essential in exposition. Through application we are able to span the gap between the world of the Bible and the world of today. Stott says two mistakes are often made in expository preaching.

First, there is the tendency to live on the Bible side of the chasm. This is probably the danger of the conservative preacher. He is so interested in accurately finding the message of the Bible that he may neglect to "earth" it out. He fails to build a bridge to the modern world. Such preaching may be clearly biblical, but it lacks contemporary application. Exposition without application never arrives at the doorstep of modern man. Stott's caution is of special interest to me. A theological conservative myself, I have been guilty too often of failure to adequately apply the message of the Bible to man where he is today.

On the other hand, there is the mistake of living on the contemporary side of the chasm. Too often liberal preachers are very contemporary but lack a biblical base. The liberal may give an up-to-date picture of contemporary life but fail to communicate an authoritative preaching truth to his congregation. Such preaching demonstrates a knowledge of what the problems are. What is lacking is an ability to give God's fresh Word as a viable solution to those problems.[31]

Stott has an excellent discussion of ways in which the expository preacher can bridge the chasm between the world of the Bible and the world of our listeners. His fourth chapter, "Preaching as Bridge-Building," is a much-needed discussion in this area. His suggestions will help you to relate your particular message to the contemporary situation. His suggestions will enable you to "contextualize" the Word of God, as he says.[32]

Drawing from Stott's suggestions, let me give you some guidelines to help you better understand contemporary man. The daily newspaper will keep you abreast of events transpiring in the world.

31. Stott, p. 138.
32. Ibid.

The wise preacher will have a Bible in one hand and the newspaper in the other. One or two good weekly magazines will give you a broad view of contemporary society. I find book reviews and reviews of plays, current music, and so on to be informative. Some awareness of the books people are reading and the music they are listening to will make the preacher sensitive to the contemporary situation. I might not go quite as far as Stott does in what the preacher needs to do to be contemporary. My personal views of biblical separation preclude attendance at some forms of entertainment. But one may be aware of contemporary thinking by reading widely. In recent years I have read more in secular fields. This has given me a better insight into where people are living today. I do agree with the German theologian Tholuck, who says, "A sermon ought to have heaven for its father and the earth for its mother."[33]

THE HOLY SPIRIT AND APPLICATION

The expository preacher has a powerful ally as he seeks to creatively communicate God's Word to the man in the pew. He has been promised the assistance of the Holy Spirit. This feature of the expository preacher's work separates him from other forms of communication. Beyond question the modern preacher of the Word is facing what appear to be insurmountable difficulties. He is preaching to people who are accustomed to well-trained, fluent, polished communicators on television and radio. He is also trying to communicate to people who may have very little Bible understanding or background. Much of the terminology of Scripture may be strange or foreign to them. In his own strength the preacher may yield to despair.

Some even go so far as to suggest that Bible preaching is irrelevant in today's world. Expository preachers are sometimes charged with answering questions no one is asking. One answer to this charge is, we are answering questions people *should* be asking. Yet, I am not so sure the charge is actually true. People are indeed asking the questions we are answering; they are just asking them in different words. Further, through intelligent, exciting, contemporary preaching of the Bible we can elicit from our hearers a desire to hear answers to the right questions.

The role of the Holy Spirit in Bible preaching solves many of these problems. He can arouse in the hearts of the listeners deep desires to know the truth. The Holy Spirit has been given by our Lord

33. Ibid., p. 150.

to bring men to an awareness of their sinfulness, the adequacy of the work of Christ, and the desirability of salvation through Him. This supernatural work of the Holy Spirit characterized the preaching of the New Testament preachers. The power of the Holy Spirit makes preaching effective and applicable. Paul states in 1 Thessalonians 1:5, "For our gospel came not unto you in word only, but also in power, and in the Holy Ghost, and in much assurance."

Through the years of my preaching ministry I have been pleased and pleasantly surprised at the effectiveness of Bible exposition. I have found that expository sermons deal with many difficult problems at the same time. Very often after a service, individuals speak to me personally about definite needs being met in their lives by the sermon, and I am not even aware that that particular need was discussed in the message. I can only assume that the Holy Spirit takes the preaching of the Word and applies timeless truths in a practical way to the lives of those helped.

We must do everything we can to enhance the practical nature of our sermons. But we must also be keenly aware that we do not preach in our own skill and energies. The Holy Spirit powerfully applies the Word when a preacher preaches.

Our goal in preaching is to lead our people to the point of obedience to the Word. We are to interpret the Scripture so as to capture its practical and devotional nature and bring the life changing truths found there to bear upon the daily lives and needs of our hearers. If our sermon preparation can produce sermons that will accomplish this goal, then there is importance and meaning to what we do. Our goal is to produce Christlike character in the lives of our people. A young Chinese student became interested in the study of the Bible. As a result, he received Jesus as his Savior. He continued to study his Bible avidly. He was asked by a friend how he was getting along in his Bible study. He replied, "I am now reading the Bible and behaving it."[34]

We desire our people to read the Bible and behave it.

34. Jensen, p. 116.

4

Organizing the Expository Sermon

If we have done our exposition work correctly, we have before us the necessary data with which to build a good, effective, expository sermon—material that can be put together to present a message from God to the hearts of our people. Analysis is not the end of our work, however.

We must now turn our attention to synthesis. Synthesis puts the pieces of the passage back together in an orderly, systematic way.

In the previous chapter we talked about the importance of applying the message to the people. We want to deliver what we have learned from the Scripture passage to our congregation. The timeless truths found in the passage must be related as clearly as possible to our people. Good sermon organization will help accomplish this purpose.

As we begin this discussion on organization I want to include a word of caution. A sameness in sermon organization can be a hindrance in conveying the message. Let the material discussed in this chapter be a guideline for your sermon preparation, but do not allow it to keep you from using different approaches from time to time. Vary the kind of points you use in your sermons. At times you may even want to dramatize certain passages of Scripture. Do not become predictable in your preaching. We only want to establish good *principles* of sermon organization. Always be aware of the need to approach your Scripture passage from a variety of angles.

Good organization is one secret of a good sermon. If you organize your message well, you will be far ahead in your attempt to get that message over to your people. Blackwood says, "If a man did not know how to preach, he might choose a paragraph which is pure gold, and yet bring out a sorry substitute for a sermon. Like Aaron, the would-be biblical preacher might complain: "I cast it into the fire, and there came out this calf!" (Exodus 32:24).[1] Don't take your Bible bullets and toss them at your congregation. Organize them, then systematically fire them. You will be pleased at the effectiveness of your fire.

In the preparation of this chapter I discovered six steps in organizing the results of exposition into an expository sermon form. Those steps are: unifying, outlining, amplifying, illustrating, introducing, and concluding. Doing the necessary work through this process will organize your material into an attractive, usable means with which to communicate God's Word.

Unifying

DETERMINING THE CENTRAL THEME

Most experts on formal speech preparation strongly emphasize the importance of having a central subject. Some refer to the subject as the main object of the talk. Others call it the central idea; still others, the theme of the speech. Emory A. Griffin, in his volume *The Mind Changers,* says, "Is it wise to present *this main point* at the start of the message, or would we be better off to wait until the conclusion? We'd do well to follow the advice of a successful country preacher. When asked the secret of his success he replied, 'It's simple. I tell them what I'm going to say. I say it. Then I tell them what I've said.' Let people know where you are headed right from the start. This way they will have a mental hook on which to hang all the illustrations and evidence you can muster to support your thesis. If they don't know where you are headed, they might unconsciously twist an example you give and see it as bolstering a different point of view."[2]

Those who have written in the field of sermon preparation have

1. Andrew Blackwood, *Preaching from the Bible* (New York: Abingdon, 1941), p. 99.
2. Emory A. Griffin, *The Mind Changers* (Wheaton, Ill.: Tyndale, 1976), p. 134.

almost unanimously taken the same position. For instance, Farris D. Whitesell, in his book *Power in Expository Preaching,* says, "The theme is the whole sermon in a nutshell. It is a one-sentence statement of the content of the message."[3] A good sermon must have a one-sentence statement that summarizes the whole thought of the Scripture passage being preached.

In my research for this book I made a startling discovery. As I talked to various preachers who are quite proficient in sermon preparation I discovered very, very few of them ever write out a one-sentence statement that summarizes the subject of their sermon. In my own sermon preparation I very rarely do what most of the experts recommend.

Perhaps this is because stating the main subject of a Scripture passage may be the most difficult area of sermon preparation. John Broadus, in his marvelous volume *The Preparation and Delivery of Sermons,* says, "To state one's central idea as the heart of the sermon is not always easy, especially in textual and expository preaching."[4] Those who have been doing regular sermon preparation for any length of time have found his statement to be true. To do the necessary word study, gather the needed background data, and study the contextual considerations is not difficult. But to pull together in one succinct statement the essence of a paragraph of Scripture can be a most rigorous assignment. One is forced to carefully think through what he has actually discovered in Scripture in order to find the unifying idea in the passage.

In many, many passages of Scripture there is not an apparent central idea or subject. Most pastors I know are extremely busy. They are preaching several times within one week. That demand places severe strains upon the time available for sermon preparation, and most find it difficult to find time to think through each sermonic passage in this manner.

Another reason we may neglect stating a theme is that we are lazy. After many years of expository sermon preparation, my observation is that a central idea can indeed be found in a passage of

---

3. Farris D. Whitesell, *Power in Expository Preaching* (Old Tappan, N.J.: Revell, 1963), p. 60.
4. John A. Broadus, *The Preparation and Delivery of Sermons* (New York: Harper, 1926), p. 52.

Scripture, however difficult the search may be. There are but few exceptions. If we will take the time to give our best thought to the search, we can find what that unifying subject is. Broadus says to find a central idea is not easy. But he also says, "The achievement is worth the effort. Even when a text presents several ideas, all of which should be incorporated in the sermon, it is desirable to find for them some bond of unity, some primary idea that will serve as focus or axis or orbit. One may fix attention on one of the ideas as the subject and consider the others in relation to it."[5] We must take the time to think through our Scripture passage with enough thoroughness to be able to determine the subject.

Perhaps many good preachers have become so accustomed to grasping the essence of the passage mentally that they have moved beyond the point of writing down the thesis. What I am suggesting is that determining the central theme of a passage of Scripture has become second nature to good preachers. I hope I am correct in this. If I am not, then many of us must be properly chastised and get about the business of finding the central idea of the passage of Scripture from which we propose to preach.

THE IMPORTANCE OF THE SUBJECT

"The proposition deserves more attention than is given by many preachers. It is a statement of the subject as the preacher proposes to develop it. It is subject and predicate. The subject answers the question, what is the subject about? The proposition answers the question, what is the sermon? Its form should be one complete declarative sentence, simple, clear, and cogent."[6] As you look at the Scripture paragraph from which you intend to preach, seek to summarize in a brief, pointed sentence what the paragraph is about. Try to write down its meaning. Many times your previous reading and analyzing of the passage will have given you sufficient clues to pick up the subject quickly. The recurrence of words may be the clue for which you are looking. Many times there will occur a sentence that is the nucleus of the passage. In your own words write down that sentence.

Having a clearly stated subject in mind will avoid a frequently

5. Ibid.
6. Ibid., p. 54.

heard criticism of expository sermons. Those who criticize the expository method say an expository sermon has no discernible structure. There is no clear-cut beginning. The points are not carefully prepared. There is no discernible conclusion. The critics charge an expository sermon is actually a combination of two or three or four or more little sermonettes rather haphazardly tied together with no obvious relation between them. Some expository efforts are done in this manner. This lack of careful organization and presentation of Bible exposition quite understandably creates in the minds of some who listen the impression that the sermon is a rambling, structureless, never-ending message. We need to avoid this at all costs. The main thrust of the passage must be made unmistakably clear.

One should make the effort to determine the central theme of a passage of Scripture because that discipline gives the preacher himself a better understanding of the truths he will be sharing with his people. Robinson says, "An exegete does not understand the passage until he can state its subject and complement exactly. While other questions emerge in the struggle to understand the meaning of a Biblical writer, the two—what is the author talking about and what is he saying about what he is talking about—are fundamental."[7] The subject sentence will crystallize in the preacher's mind the single, controlling idea of the passage. "A sermon should be a bullet not a buckshot. Ideally each sermon is the explanation, interpretation, or application of a single dominant idea supported by other ideas, all drawn from one passage or several passages of Scripture."[8]

Stating the subject of the passage in a clear sentence will also be of great help to those who hear your message. They will be better able to understand what you are saying. People who come to listen to you have given you some of their valuable time. They deserve to have a well-arranged, clearly thought-through message. The effort will be worthwhile.

Writing out a subject sentence will also assist you in cutting out unnecessary material from your sermon. More than likely you will have at the conclusion of your exposition more material than you can possibly put together into one sermon. You may have enough information for several sermons. You cannot include all the material you

7. Haddon W. Robinson, *Biblical Preaching* (Grand Rapids: Baker, 1980), p. 41.
8. Ibid., p. 33.

have found. Do not weary your people by giving them every minute detail. You may go into so much detail that you miss the controlling purpose of the Scripture paragraph. Having a well-thought-through theme sentence will aid you in removing unnecessary material. Whatever the length of your sermon, you will not likely be able to do justice to every facet of the Scripture passage. Find the central theme. Use those parts of the paragraph that make that theme the clearest and most emphatic.

TESTS FOR SERMON SUBJECTS

Koller has given a series of tests for the subject of a Scripture paragraph. First, he suggests that the theme should indicate the course of the discussion that is to follow. The subject is a promise that the discourse must actually fulfill. Second, a good theme should be a generalization including the timeless, universal truth of the passage. Third, most of the time the subject should be a simple sentence. Fourth, the central idea should be very clear. Fifth, the theme should comprehend the entire thought of the message. The gist of the sermon must be given in one sentence. Sixth, the subject should be important enough to deserve the elaboration that follows in the main body of the sermon. Seventh, the theme should be sermonic in character, calling for some response.[9]

The central theme or subject of your Scripture passage will assist you as you organize your entire message. A sense of direction will be given to everything that follows: As we shall see in the chapter on outlining, the main points should actually be found in the Scripture passage used. When you have determined the subject of the passage, you will find you can much easier arrange the main points of the message. The introduction of the sermon is easier to put together when you know where you are going from the outset. The conclusion of the message can be built more effectively. We know where we are going. We know where we have been. Now, in conclusion, we tie the whole message together. Koller suggests that the thesis of the sermon is actually the conclusion in reverse. The theme looks ahead, anticipating the conclusion. The conclusion points back to the thesis.[10]

9. Charles W. Koller, *Expository Preaching Without Notes* (Grand Rapids: Baker, 1961), pp. 72-74.

As you begin to put your Scripture passage back together, putting the details into a well-balanced, logical, orderly message, be very careful to do your homework in the area of determining the theme of the passage.

THE PURPOSE

We must not confuse the subject, or theme, of the passage with the purpose of the message. The effective preacher must know what is the purpose of his message. The purpose of your message is what you desire in terms of audience response. You know what the passage is about. You know its central thrust. What do you want your listeners to do about the subject? This is extremely important. If the preacher does not know what he wants the people to do about the message, how can he expect them to do anything? I have heard many sermons that never gave the faintest notion to those of us who listened what the preacher wanted us to do. The people must know what they are being called to do, if they are to respond favorably.

When I think of the purpose of a message, I think in terms of several matters. Sometimes my purpose is to inform my people about certain vital doctrines in the Scriptures. I inform them about these doctrines in order to lead them to do one of several things. I may want them to determine to be more grateful to God for what He has done for them. I may want them to build these truths into their daily habit patterns. I may want them to communicate these truths to others. At other times I am seeking to comfort my people with a positive message from God's Word. The purpose of such a sermon is to encourage and to strengthen them in their times of need. Sometimes I want to challenge them with the call of Scripture to total surrender or complete dedication. When I preach, my purpose takes a variety of directions. I am seeking to inform or to inspire. My purpose is to motivate or to challenge. I am trying to encourage or to rebuke. Though you may not put down your purpose in writing every time you prepare a sermon, you should have that purpose clearly in mind.

Early in your message let your people know how you are expecting them to respond. Keep your purpose in mind throughout the

10. Ibid., p. 74.

arrangement of your sermon. Drive toward the conclusion. As you conclude the message you will become very personal in your appeal to the people. A message from the Scripture is not merely a discourse that is to be received as information, after which the people are dismissed. Preaching calls for a response. Give the people a challenge. No paragraph of Scripture is without a personal appeal to the heart. Find the appeal and press it home. The people will be blessed as a result.

THE TITLE

I mention the title of an expository sermon at this point merely because to do so fits in better here than other places. I am not suggesting you must have your title at this early point of your sermon organization. You may not find your title until the end of the message. Perhaps the title will come to you in the midst of your study. During your expository work the title of the message may flash into your mind. We are not so much interested in when we get the title as we are in the reason for having a title. The title of a message differs both from the subject and the purpose of a sermon. The title is primarily intended to get attention. You are seeking to arouse interest on the part of those who may hear your message. Perhaps you may list the sermon title in a weekly church ad. For many years I listed my weekly sermon titles in the church paper. Because of earlier printing deadlines I have not done this in recent years. When I was able to do so I found the sermon titles often stimulated interest in the coming sermon. The stating of a title at the beginning of a message can help you gain the attention of your listeners at the moment of delivery. These are primary reasons for having a title to your message.

A sermon title should be brief. "Seventeen Reasons Why the Modern Church is Not Getting the Job Done as It Should Be Getting It Done" is not a good sermon title. Try to catch the gist of your sermon in a brief, catchy title. Avoid sensational titles. Avoid the ridiculous. Such titles as "Seven Dips in a Muddy Pond' (a sermon on Namaan, the leper) really become absurd. Do not promise more than you can deliver in a message. Some preachers have lost credibility because the substance of their sermon did not fulfill the enormous claims of the title.

In the next section we will move specifically into the basic ingredients of good sermonic organization. We will discuss the main
points of the expository sermon outline. The main points will be easier
to develop if you will give attention to the matter of the theme sentence.

Outlining

Rousseau, describing the unorganized love letter of a young man
to his girl friend, said, "He had begun without knowing what he was
going to say, and he finished without knowing what he had uttered."[11]
This statement could well describe many sermons. Without a clear,
logical outline a sermon does not have the effect and power it could
have. Herbert Spencer said, "When a man's knowledge is not in order,
the more of it he has, the greater will be his confusion of thought."[12]

I consider outlining perhaps the most important part of sermon
organization. We have already discussed the value of identifying the
unifying theme of the Scripture passage. A good outline will enhance
the ability of the preacher to communicate the central theme. Outlines
are very much like road maps. They allow us to view where we are
going and keep us on the proper road as we journey toward our desired
destination. They also may be compared to an arrow. The shaft of
the arrow must be straight. The point must be penetrating. The feathers
must be just in the right proportion to steady the arrow in flight.[13]
Outlines are the burrs that lodge themselves in the minds of our
listeners.[14]

ADVANTAGES OF AN OUTLINE

Developing a sermon outline enables the preacher to give structure to his message. Too often the preacher takes a text, departs
therefrom, and goes everywhere preaching the gospel. This is the

11. Josh McDowell, Syllabus on Communication and Persuasion. Copyright 1983 by Josh
McDowell.
12. Ibid., p. 28.
13. Koller, p. 41.
14. John Phillips, *One Hundred Sermon Outlines from the New Testament* (Chicago:
Moody, 1979), n.p.

danger of a sermon that has no points.[15] A good outline keeps a preacher on course throughout the message. An outline enables him to better summarize what he has said for a final impression upon the listeners.

A clear outline also serves as a kind of guide for the listener. As the message is delivered the hearer can follow the logical unfolding of the message better if there is a clear outline throughout.

Another benefit of the sermon outline is that it gives a sense of pace to the sermon. The message is going somewhere. The sermon is taking a logical step-by-step journey through a passage of Scripture. An outline enables you to move toward an effective climax. As you build your sermon outline you will keep in mind the importance of your points moving toward a climax. This will give a sense of expectancy and anticipation to your sermons.

There are several purposes of an outline for an expository sermon. The outline makes clear in the preacher's understanding the relationships between the parts of the sermon. He is able to move from the introduction into the main points. Each point can be related to another as he unfolds the main theme of the sermon.

An outline also helps the preacher to see his sermon in its entirety. It gives to the preacher a sense of the unity of the message.

As the preacher prepares his message the outline will assist him in properly arranging his material. If the job of exposition has been done correctly, he has an abundance of material that can be used in the sermon. How is this material to be arranged? Where does each piece of information best fit in the message? A good outline will answer these and many other questions.[16]

GET YOUR POINTS FROM THE PASSAGE

In expository sermon preparation the main points should be drawn from the passage. This is one of the distinguishing characteristics of expository sermons. An outline is not imposed upon the Scripture passage. Rather, the outline naturally emerges from the material of the passage at hand. The object of these points, or divisions, in the message is to make clear the central idea of your Scripture.

15. Donald Demaray, *An Introduction to Homiletics* (Grand Rapids: Baker, 1974), p. 78.
16. Robinson, p. 128.

To get your main points from the passage itself also solves the matter of the number of points you will use. The number of points in a sermon has been a matter often discussed in books on sermon preparation. There are those who are rather rigid in this respect. Some strongly urge that the sermon must have three points. The old joke, he had three points and a poem, is characteristic of many preachers. There does seem to be a sense of balance and beauty about a sermon with three points. But the preacher must not fall into a numerical trap. The number of points will vary according to the substance of the passage. When you get your main points from the Scripture passage you may have two or three or more. Should you exceed four points in your message, you might be using too much Scripture for one sermon. The number of points is not an essential matter. Just be sure the passage itself gives you those points.

Do not force points from your Scripture. Martyn Lloyd-Jones tells the story of a preacher who was enamored with the passage concerning the woman at the well. On an occasion he preached on the text, "And Balaam arose early and sat on his ass." He divided the text into these divisions: 1. A Good Trait in a Bad Character. "Balaam arose." 2. The Antiquity of Saddlery. "And sat on his ass." 3. And, "In Conclusion, a Few Remarks Concerning the Woman at the Well."[17]

The matter of when to get your sermon outline needs also to be considered. I have found that the outline may come at any given point in my study of the passage. Sometimes at the very beginning of my reading of the Scripture passage the points will quickly emerge. This always produces a very, very good feeling! At other times I do not immediately see the main points of the passage. Determining the central thrust and supporting points of the passage takes longer. Therefore, I am unable to draw from the passage the main points for a while.

Some preachers seem more gifted than others in being able to divide a passage into its main divisions. Martin Lloyd-Jones discusses the obvious gift of Alexander Maclaren, the famous Baptist expositor in England. Lloyd-Jones says that Maclaren seemed to have a kind of golden hammer in his hand with which he could tap a text, and

17. D. Martyn Lloyd-Jones, *Preaching and Preachers* (Grand Rapids: Zondervan, 1971), p. 208.

immediately the text would divide itself into sharp, crisp divisions.[18] Others have to work very hard at developing the main points of the message.

A great deal of your time may be spent in getting the main points for the sermon. Harold Ockenga says, "I spend the most time on my outline, so that it is logical, alliterative, parallelistic, and easy to remember."[19] I also spend a good bit of time in this particular effort.

There is the danger you will spend so much time trying to get your points that you get yourself into a mental paralysis. Your inability to determine the main divisions of the text can so frustrate you that you become nervous and tense. When that happens much time can be wasted trying to find an outline. I would recommend that you not stop your study when you are unable to adequately determine the main points of the message. Continue to study. Move on through the various stages of your preparation. The main points may very well emerge at some later stage of preparation. If they do not, they may surface during those times when your subconscious mind is working on the message. In our section on incubation I will share with you some suggestions to help you break the mental tangle that sometimes comes during preparation.

QUALITIES OF A GOOD OUTLINE

Let me give you some qualities of a good outline. First, the main points should have a parallel structure. Do not have one kind of sentence arrangement for one point and another kind for another point. Keep your main points parallel in structure. This will give a sense of unity and symmetry.

Each of your points in the outline should be mutually exclusive. There should be no overlapping. Do not include material in one point that has already been included in a previous point. Keep your points related to the central theme, but be sure each is independent of the others in content and development of the central theme.

Kaiser has also suggested that each main point should avoid the use of the past tense verb and all proper names. He suggests that the

18. Ibid., p. 207.
19. Demaray, p. 84.

points should be put in the present tense as much as possible.[20] This gives a sense of application to those who listen. Keeping your points in the present tense will help you get from the Bible world to the world of your listeners. This may not always be possible to do. Kaiser's suggestion does have real merit, however. This can help your message have a more contemporary ring to it.

State the main points in complete sentences. Avoid lengthy sentences. Make each point as concise and complete as possible.

The main points of the sermon should have a gradual heightening of interest as they proceed. This can be accomplished in several ways. Do not allow yourself to become unduly occupied with any single point. One could easily preach a sermon from each of the main points of a message. You must avoid the temptation to get so involved in any single point that you fail to give adequate attention to the others. In the earlier years of my ministry I would become so involved in the first point (sometimes even in the introduction!) that I spent most of my time there and had very little time to deal with the remaining points. This is fatal from several perspectives. A sense of movement in your sermon is hindered. This produces a slackening of interest in the message. In watching my audience as I preach, if I see movement, and other indications of inattention, I may well be saying the same thing over and over again. This is a signal for me to move on to my next point.

Your main points should move toward a climax. Keep ever before you the main theme the points are intended to develop. Normally, you will want to reach your climax at the latter part of the message. The Scripture passage will probably be so arranged that you can easily do this. If the material in a particular Scripture paragraph follows a logical arrangement, a strong climax may be reached. Following the points as they emerge from the Scripture passage itself should assist you in building your message to a climax.

Each main point should be a statement, not a question. The points in your outline are intended to answer questions, not ask them .Give your people answers to the questions that normally arise from the Scripture passage at hand.

What we have said about the main points of a sermon outline

20. Walter C. Kaiser, Jr., *Toward an Exegetical Theology* (Grand Rapids: Baker, 1982), p. 152.

may also be said about the subpoints under each main point. Generally, I follow the same procedure in building my subpoints as I do my main points. They also must have parallel structure. They should be mutually exclusive. Each subpoint should be an unfolding of the main point.

DANGERS IN OUTLINING

There are some dangers to be avoided in outlining. Do not allow your outline to become so noticeable that it detracts from the substance of what you are saying. Your outline is the skeleton of the sermon. Be careful that the bones of your message do not protrude to the point that the meat of the message is missed. Although a sermon outline should be clear and appealing, avoid the temptation to make it overly clever and sensational. You may acquire a reputation as a skillful outliner but will not give as much practical help to your people as you desire.

An outline may be imposed upon a Scripture passage. Earlier in this chapter we stated that the main points should be drawn from the passage of Scripture itself. If you have a propensity toward a certain number of points, you may impose more points upon an outline than you need. Often in my exposition of a passage of Scripture I become aware that the passage does not lend itself to as many points as I had originally thought. Try to faithfully reflect in your outline only what the Scripture passage itself will allow.

There is room for a great deal of variety and originality in the arranging of sermon outlines. Some outlines are like ladders. Each point moves to the next one like the rungs of a ladder. Other sermon outlines are like a beautiful diamond. The single, central idea of the passage is approached from several angles so that each facet of the idea's beauty may be seen. Still other sermon outlines are like a skyrocket. The passage begins on the ground, rises to magnificent heights, bursts into pieces, then gracefully comes to earth again.[21]

THE KEY WORD

One of the most helpful suggestions in developing sermon outlines is found in Whitesell's book *Power in Expository Preaching*.

21. John R.W. Stott, *Between Two Worlds* (Grand Rapids: Eerdmans, 1982), p. 229.

Whitesell recommends the use of what he calls a key word. The key word is a plural noun that tells what the main points of the message are. Using a lead-in sentence around this plural noun, the main points of your message may be arranged. This will enable you to have parallel structure, to state your main points in sentences, and tie them all together in an orderly, logical manner.

Whitesell gives several values of the key word concept. First, the key word enables you to classify your main points by keeping them in one category. Second, this plural noun points you in the direction you intend to follow throughout the development of your message. Third, a sense of unity is given to your sermon. Fourth, the key word is an aid in the construction of your main points in a parallel manner. Fifth, this allows you to test your main points to see if they fit with the other points in your outline. Sixth, the main points of your sermon are tied together. Seventh, the key word is an aid to you as you memorize the main points of your sermon.[22]

Koller also has a helpful discussion on the key word. The key word is a word that characterizes each of the main points and holds the structure together. According to Koller, the great value of the key word is that a corridor is opened down the length of the sermon structure. The key word is always a noun or a noun form of a verb or an adjective.[23] On pages 53-55 of Koller's book *Expository Preaching Without Notes,* an extensive list of possible key words is given. You will find this list to be very helpful. For instance, in your sermon you may use the word *marks* as your key word. In your message you may discuss the marks of a growing Christian life. Or, you might use the word *phases* in a sermon on the phases in the development of a Christian life. Avoid the use of *things.* This word is much too general. Seek for a specific key word that can help you move into the main points of your message.

The outline of your message is an extremely important part of its organization. Good organization requires the development of your main points before you add argumentation, amplification, illustration, and application to your message. A good, neat outline enables you to place all of these added ingredients into your message in the most appropriate and beneficial places.

22. Whitesell, p. 60.
23. Koller, pp. 52-53.

ALLITERATION

The use of alliteration in outlining sermons is a very controversial subject. Many of the finest teachers of homiletics frown upon its use. On the other hand, many effective expository preachers both past and present have used the method of alliteration. By alliteration we mean the successive use or frequent recurrence of the same initial letter or sound at the beginning of two or more words.

Alliteration has had a prominent place in literature, especially in poetry and with certain prominent figures of literary history. Among these are Chaucer, Spenser, Swinburne, and others. Certain phrases that occur in common speech have come out of the use of alliteration. Some of those are "might and main," "life and liberty," "wrath and wickedness." There is even some evidence of the use of alliteration in the Greek words Paul uses in the closing verses of Romans 1.

There are several objections to the use of alliteration in sermon outlining. Those who use alliteration sometimes demonstrate a tendency to manipulate the subject matter in order to make the content fit a desired alliterative outline. When this occurs alliteration can be a hindrance to preaching the truth. Broadus points out that alliteration, if used too freely, can tend to stiffness or to monotony. Broadus states that a constant succession of smooth and graceful sentences can sooner or later become very monotonous. In defense of alliteration, however, Broadus does say that sentences are most eloquent when they are smooth and flowing.[24]

Also, one may become so addicted to the use of alliteration that the outline becomes much too burdensome. Many preachers who get overly interested in alliteration not only alliterate the main points, they also alliterate the subpoints. In addition, they use alliteration in the points under the subpoints. Further, they use alliteration in individual sentences. This can be very annoying for those who must listen.

Those who oppose the use of alliteration give no adequate argument against its use when the method is used properly. There are several good purposes for alliteration. First, an alliterative outline may often be fitted to good interpretation. I have found many times that the natural flow of my Scripture passage lends itself to an allit-

24. Broadus, p. 273.

erative outline. This is not always true. But when it occurs I see no good reason to avoid its use.

An alliterative outline is a useful aid to the preacher's memory. The whole task of memorizing outlines is greatly simplified. If the main points can be alliterative in nature, and if they come from the Scripture passage itself, your outline can more easily be recalled as you proceed through your sermon. When done well, good alliteration is conducive to sound Bible exposition.

There is another very positive reason to use alliteration. Alliteration has a way of making the main points of your sermon stick. Impressions are created upon the minds of your listeners that will not be quickly forgotten. I can remember the basic outlines of literally hundreds of sermons I have heard other preachers deliver, because they are alliterative in nature.

If you decide to use alliteration, guard against forcing or inaccurate presentation of the substance of your preaching paragraph. I see nothing wrong with searching for alliteration. There is no good reason in my opinion for rejecting the method if it can be used for better reasons than a demonstration of the preacher's ingenuity and cleverness.

If you decide to use alliteration in outlining your sermons, please use alliteration well. Nothing is as poor as a poor alliterative outline. Let me give you one or two examples of poor alliteration in sermon outlining. Stibbs gives an outline for Matthew 24:35-44. The passage is outlined as follows:

1. A Pertinent Contrast
2. A Pointed Comparison
3. A Paradoxical Crisis
4. Our Prospect Comparable
5. The Practical Challenge

Several flaws are apparent in this outline. The first three points parallel one another; the last two are not parallel. The first three points use adjectives that begin with a *p*. The fourth point uses a noun that begins with a *p* and a verb that begins with a *c*, in contrast to the nouns that begin with *c* in the first three points. Then, the fifth point jumps back to the structure of the first three points. The fourth point does not seem to fit. This is poor alliterative outlining.

Another example of a poor use of alliteration is found in Kaiser's outline on Nehemiah 6:1-19. He uses a four point outline:

1. A God-Given Sense of Direction, vv. 1-4
2. A God-Given Spirit of Determination, vv. 5-9
3. A God-Given Heart of Discernment, vv. 10-14
4. A God-Given Demonstration of Approval, vv. 15-19

Just a quick glance at this outline shows its inadequacies. The first two points are parallel in structure. The third point has no alliteration consistent with the words *sense* and *spirit* in the previous two points. The fourth point is even worse. The outline continues by using a word that begins with a *d* as in the three previous points but is out of place in the sentence structure.

Learn to use good alliteration. If the alliterative word in your first point is a noun, then let the alliterative word be a noun in the succeeding points. If you use an alliterative verb in your first point, let the alliterative words be verbs in the succeeding points. I have come to view alliteration in two ways. "Front-door alliteration" means beginning a word with the same letter, even the same first syllable. Let me give two examples of front-door alliteration, using the beginning letter:

Sermon Outline on John 3
1. The Must of the New Birth
2. The Mystery of the New Birth
3. The Means of the New Birth

Sermon Outline on James 3:1-12
1. Directive Nature of the Tongue
2. Destructive Nature of the Tongue
3. Deceptive Nature of the Tongue

An example of an outline that has alliteration using the first syllable is:

Sermon Outline on 1 Peter 1:13-21
1. The Imperatives of Pilgrim Living
2. The Implications of Pilgrim Living

By "back-door alliteration" I mean using words that have similar endings. Let me give you two examples here. In a sermon on substitutes for Christ, taken from Colossians 2:8-23, I organized the verses around four main points. I presented four main substitutes people place before Christ. They are:

1. Intellectualism (vv. 8-10)
2. Ritualism (vv. 11-17)
3. Mysticism (vv. 18-19)
4. Legalism (vv. 20-23)

Notice that each of the words closes with the same syllable, *-ism*. In a sermon taken from Titus 2:11-15, I used an outline giving three reasons God's grace is amazing:

God's grace is amazing because it brings:

1. Salvation (v. 11)
2. Education (v. 12)
3. Anticipation (v. 13)

Each word in my outline concludes with the syllable, *-tion*.

I want to emphasize again that I am not insisting alliteration be used in your sermon outlining. I am simply saying that the abuse of alliteration is not an adequate reason to reject its use altogether. Further, I am urging that you use good alliteration if you intend to use it at all. If the alliteration comes naturally from the Scripture passage, do not hesitate to use it. If alliterative points come from the passage without being forced, I see no good reason to avoid it.

OUTLINE ARRANGEMENT

I follow a fairly common method of arranging my outline. I begin with my introduction. Then I arrange the main points by Roman numerals (I, II, III, etc.). Under my main points I use for my subpoints

A, B, C, and so on. For the material under my subpoints I use numbers 1, 2, 3, and so on. I indent my subpoints under my main points. Then, I indent my supporting material under each one of my subpoints. This gives me a neat, easy-to-read arrangement for my sermon outline. A typical point with its subpoints and supporting materials looks like this:

Mark, #38

GUILTY OF LOVE IN THE FIRST DEGREE
Mark 14:53-65; 15:1-20.

INTRODUCTION:
Many famous trials: Scopes monkey trial; Nuremberg trials; Patti Hearst. Most famous—trial of Jesus. That day, not only Jesus on trial but whole world.
Actually, 2 trials: *religious; civil.* 6 parts: (1) Before *Annas.* Power behind scenes. Head of religious mafia. Rich from Temple shops. (2) *Caiaphas.* High Priest. (3) *Sanhedrin.* Seventy-one leaders of Jewish nation. Could try cases, not execute penalty. Not a court of justice—a slaughterhouse. (4) *Pilate.* (5)*Herod.* (6) *Pilate* again.
Lawyers studied, called mockery of justice. Filled with illegalities: (1) *Place.* Only in Hall of Hewn Stones, Temple. (2) *Period of time.* At night, during feast. No day intervened. (3) *Proceedings.* Judge prosecuted. Two or three witnesses agree. Someone speak for accused.
Really, a kangaroo court. Reason: "envy," v. 10. Not a trial—a plot. Judicial murder. Condemned before His trial. Convicted before case ever heard. Actually, put them on trial for all time.
The Lord on Trial—
I.   Before the *HEBREWS* 14:53-65.
     As Jesus stands before Jewish leaders we see—
         A. The Lord *accused.* "False witnesses."
             1. Sought witnesses against Him. Couldn't get their testimonies to agree. Demolished one another.
             2. V. 58. Misquoted statement of Jesus. *John 2:19.* Temple not stone and timber—His own body.
             3. Could have found some witnesses: *leper; blind; lame; dead.* His enemies could have testified: Judas, "innocent blood"; Pilate's wife, "this just man."
             4. Anyone here give testimony? Found Him faithful or unfaithful?

B. The Lord *arraigned*. "Blasphemy."
   1. Caiaphas. Not interested in facts. Should have been. To lead people to look for Messiah. He to enter Holy of Holies each year for people.
   2. He takes matters into own hands. Plays his trump card. Puts Jesus on sacred oath "I am." He makes definite claim to be Messiah.
   3. High Priest—fakes anguish, tears clothes. Last of human high priests. Before day out another cloth torn—veil in Temple, top to bottom. Men now able to enter presence of God.

TRANSITIONAL STATEMENTS

Transitional statements are very important to a good outline. A good transition alerts the listener to the fact that the preacher is moving from one thought to another. Most preachers have given too little attention to transitions. They are often an afterthought. But a good sermon will have clear, smooth transitions between its major sections. Transitions give evidence that the preacher clearly understands each section of his sermon and also knows how one section moves logically to another.

Transitions demonstrate the logical relationships between the divisions of your sermon outline. Try to state the transitional statements you will make between your points. This will help you test the structure of your outline. If your points follow a logical sequence, you should be able to move easily from one to the other. Should you encounter trouble connecting each major division of your message, your difficulty may be a caution that something has gone wrong.

Transitions fulfill two primary functions. First, they assist the preacher in testing his logic. Second, they aid the listeners in their understanding of the preacher's logic.[25]

Broadus says that the transitions from one part of a sermon to the next are best when they are least noticeable. He further states that ideal transitional statements are those that enable the constituent parts of your sermon to fit together perfectly.[26]

25. Milton Dickens, *Speech: Dynamic Communication* (New York: Harcourt Brace Jovanovich, 1954), p. 141.
26. Broadus, p. 119.

Usually transitions can be made by a single sentence. Use some form of statement that will cause your listeners to be aware you are moving from one thought to another. Often words may be used to make the transition. Such words as *again, moreover, furthermore, in the next place* can make good transitions.

Transitions are like glue, which holds all the material of your message together. They briefly forecast the next thought, they quickly summarize the previous thought, and they show the connection of one thought to another. A transitional statement is like a sign that says, This is the way, follow me.

The transition from the introduction of your sermon to the main points is perhaps the easiest. Using the key word I have already discussed can be very helpful to you. The concluding paragraph in your introduction will move from the introductory material to the main body of the sermon. This can be done by means of a sentence using the key word that moves naturally into your main points. Vary the way you introduce each main point. I would caution against excessive use of numerical notations. Listeners very often tire of "first," "second," and "third." Instead of saying, "The second mark . . ." why not say, "The next mark . . ." or "An additional mark . . ." or "A further mark . . ."?

Transitions between the various points of your sermon can usually be very quickly made. Such words as: *next, let us consider, further, I call your attention to, in addition to,* or *consider* will move you rapidly to your next thought. These kinds of transitional statements indicate the conclusion of one point and the beginning of the next.

The transition between the main points of your message and the conclusion is also vitally important. Several words or phrases are commonly used. Some of these are: *finally, in conclusion, in summary.* These are not best. You may move into a conclusion more effectively without making the people excessively aware that the conclusion is rapidly approaching. The time will let them know you are nearing the conclusion! Try to develop new and unique ways of bringing your message to a climax and wrapping up your sermon.

The transition from your concluding remarks to the invitation you will give to the people is also an important part of your sermon. I will discuss this in some detail when we come to the chapter on concluding the sermon.

The development of your sermon outline is an essential and enjoyable part of sermon organization. Learn to outline well. Study the sermons of preachers who are gifted in outlining. Observe how they develop the main points of their message. Watch the logical flow of their main points. Test them to see if they derive their main points from the Scripture passage itself. Carefully note their transitional statements. Do not merely *read* the sermons of good preachers. *Listen* to their taped sermons or hear them in person. Carefully watch how they organize their messages.

You will spend all of your ministry working to improve the outlines of your sermons. The suggestions I have made in this section will get you started.

Amplifying

After you have unified your passage of Scripture and prepared a good, useable outline, the time has come to add supporting material to your sermon. Some refer to this as putting meat on the bones of your message. Some preachers make the mistake of giving only the bare framework of a sermon outline as the substance of their sermon. This is as unpalatable to a listener as unwanted bones in a good fish dinner. The people want and deserve more than just an outline. There must be material to support, amplify, and drive home the truths you have discovered in the Scripture.

When I move into this part of my sermon preparation I think in terms of three main ingredients for each main point—explanation, application, and illustration. Much of your explanation will be taken from the expository material you have gained during your analysis of the passage. You will want to give your people some explanation of the meaning of the passage based on word study, background information, contextual considerations, and parallel passages.

Then you will want to apply these truths, which are represented by your main points, in as persuasive a manner as possible. Several means of persuasion are available to the expository preacher. One of those is the use of the Word of God. There is persuasive power in the use of the Scripture in and of itself. The Bible has an inherent authority. Billy Graham, the man who has preached to more people than any other in the history of Christianity, is characterized by his constant use of the phrase "the Bible says." Much of Dr. Graham's effectiveness is due to the persuasive way he uses the Word of God to support the substance of his messages.

The character of the preacher himself can aid in persuasively applying the truth of the Scripture. Aristotle called this *ethos*. As the preacher delivers his message his own modesty, sincerity, intensity, and yieldedness to the authority of Scripture will substantially add to the credibility of the message. Though this does not add to the content of the message, the very sincerity of the preacher is a factor in amplifying the sermon's main points.

The appeal to reason also can add substance to your sermon. Aristotle called this *logos*. Study ways to present your material so it appeals to your people's logic.

The emotional appeal can also help you more persuasively convey your message to the people. Aristotle called this *pathos*. Be sure that there is ample emotional content in your sermon. Whitesell says that people are not moved so much by lengthy or involved arguments as they are by illustrations, humor, and emotion. He maintains that people are more likely to be moved by emotions than reason.[27]

The third ingredient of the supporting material that amplifies your main points is illustration, which we will discuss in the next section.

Just where does the preacher turn to find material that can add flesh to the bones of his sermon? Must he spin all his sermonic content from his own mind? To do so calls for a very unique ability to be creative. As Broadus says, "Originality means bringing into existence thoughts which the world never knew before, which had never arisen in any human mind. Of course, this must be very rare."[28] There are very, very few original thinkers. There are even fewer preachers who produce original material. I think often of the statement made by the beloved evangelist Vance Havner: "At the beginning of my ministry I determined I would be original or nothing. I soon found out that I was both." But the preacher can go to many sources for amplifying material.

27. Whitesell, p. 63.
28. Broadus, p. 83.

HOMILETICAL DEVICES

The preacher may make use of what Koller calls the six homi-letical devices.[29] The first is narration. In language that is picturesque, contemporary, and vivid the preacher can make a narrative section of Scripture "come alive." Let me caution you not to fall into the trap of merely retelling narrative passages of Scripture from which you preach as a regular procedure. The preacher may easily neglect to study properly by merely telling a Scripture story in his own words.

Second is the device of interpretation. This is to get at the meaning of the Scripture passage. Define the terms in the passage. Describe what is taking place.

Third, Koller mentions illustration. This device brings together all the sources of preaching material you have available to you.

Fourth is application, which we have already mentioned.

Fifth, there is the matter of argumentation. By the use of reasoning, proofs, and testimony the preacher can add helpful supporting material. The use of personal testimony is a helpful device in adding substance to your message. Paul frequently referred to his own experience with the Lord. This can certainly be overdone but at times is very appropriate and meaningful.

The sixth homiletical device is exhortation. Call the hearer to some definite course of action. This may often be used in the concluding section of your message. But as you amplify your main points there will naturally come places where exhortation can be used effectively.

OTHER SOURCES

Haddon Robinson, in his book *Biblical Preaching*, says "Supporting material is to the outline what skin is to bone or walls to the frame of a house."[30] He lists some interesting and seldom mentioned ways to add supporting material. Among those is *restatement*, giving the same idea in different words. This is a positive way to increase the clarity of your message. Restatement underscores what you are

29. Koller, p. 50.
30. Robinson, p. 137.

trying to say in the minds of your hearers.[31]

I have found *statistics* to be valuable when trying to amplify some point in a sermon. I am always on the lookout for statistics in newspapers, magazines, and books. Be careful not to overuse statistics, and be sure your statistics are correct. *Quotations* can lend strength to your main points. A quotation from a well-known person, in contemporary life or in history, can lend a sense of authority to what you are saying. I have in my own library several books of quotations. Sometimes I have even found a quotation from an unbeliever to be helpful in supporting a truth of Scripture. On occasion I have used a quotation from an unbeliever that is untrue. I have used the quote by way of contrast with the truth I am seeking to convey.

I have found the multiple approach to a Scripture passage will many times give me additional material to use. When I have exhausted every possible meaning and interpretation I can discover in the passage, the multiple approach has often given me something new.[32] The multiple approach is looking at the Scripture passage from a variety of viewpoints, for example, the viewpoint of the reader or the people who are involved. In the passage on the stoning of Stephen in Acts 8, study the passage from the viewpoint of Stephen. Look at the account from the vantage point of those who stoned him. Then, view the scene from God's point of view. You might even want to invent dialogue. Imagine what the people in the passage might have said. Let them talk to one another. Let them talk to themselves. You will be amazed at the suggestions this approach will provide for you.

During your analysis of the Scripture passage you have consulted a variety of commentaries. As you read through the commentaries you may find certain statements that amplify the truths of the passage. Make a careful note of them along the way. Underline them. Note them on the margin. Mark the location of the page in the book. When you are amplifying your sermon points refer back to them. You will find material here that can assist you in expanding the truths of your main points.

Read sermons that other men have preached on the passage under consideration. Several years ago, W. A. Criswell shared with me the most helpful homiletical key he had ever found. Criswell assigns to

31. Ibid., pp. 138-39.
32. Koller, pp. 55-56.

each of his sermon books a number. In a wide-margin Bible he lists book and page numbers beside the text for each sermon. I have been following this suggestion for many years. It has saved me hundreds of hours previously spent in searching through my sermon books. In a matter of minutes I can find every sermon I have in my library on any given passage of Scripture. I strongly recommend this method to you.

At this point you may wonder about borrowing material. May we legally and ethically use the material of another writer or preacher? The lifting of material word for word is certainly improper. When you quote another preacher or writer give proper credit. But it is proper to read the materials of others, absorb them into your own mental processes, and then use them as the Lord may lead you. Jay Adams suggests that borrowing is permissible when you give new organization, new integration, and new expression to the materials you have read. He suggests that you mix the materials through your own mind, add them to your own experiences, then give them in your own way.[33]

There are still other sources from which to draw supporting material. You can amplify the main points of your message from previous materials you have gathered. For several years I have been keeping notebooks of the sermonic preparation I have done. These notebooks are organized by books of the Bible. In them I have more information than I ever intended to use in the particular sermons I was preparing at the time. I have found this to be a very fruitful source of supporting material. Why do all the study necessary to preach expository sermons, then discard material that is not needed in a particular message at a particular time? Use whatever method or system you prefer, but keep the results of your study for future reference.

Haddon Robinson has made another good suggestion to amplify the main points of your sermon. Anticipate objections your listeners may make to the truths you present. Add your answers to those suggestions. He cautions that we should not raise objections that no one else would raise. Further, we should show respect and consideration for those who may hold views contrary to our own.[34]

33. Jay Adams, *Pulpit Speech* (Phillipsburg, N.J.: Presbyterian and Reformed, 1971), p. 15.
34. Robinson, pp. 71-72.

The preacher who does expository work will be constantly adding information to his store of knowledge. Everything he sees, reads, or hears is potential material for sermonic preparation. He is constantly filling his sermon barrel. Harper Shannon says, "This [preaching from the overflow] is an artesian well where the water flows steadily but the great reservoir of water is underneath the earth. If the well flows year in and year out in the small stream, one can rest assured that there are hundreds of thousands of gallons of water underneath the earth that are never seen. This is a good description of the process of studying to preach."[35] As the years go by the expository preacher will develop a great reservoir of sermon material. As you prepare your sermons week by week you will be able to draw from this ever-increasing supply.

This is one way the preacher can avoid the problem of being set aside in the latter years of his ministry. The preacher who maintains his study habits will have something fresh and relevant to say. He will never lack an audience.

I want to remind you about the need to eliminate from your sermon unnecessary material. Sometimes when we have worked hard to accumulate a large body of information we are loathe to exclude any of it. We must be absolutely unyielding in eliminating irrelevant content from our sermons. Any material that does not definitely amplify what we are seeking to say must be rigorously discarded. Use only the material that applies to the subject at hand. If you acquire some information so good you just must use it, file it away for ready reference. Use the extra material in a more appropriate message.

Illustrating

Probably you remember several outstanding sermons you have heard. As you reflect upon those sermons, likely you can remember the illustrations in them. The illustrations very often make the message. An effective illustration can actually save a sermon. A good illustration may be the difference between an average and an outstanding sermon.

Illustrations are mental photographs that illumine the ideas of

---

35. Harper Shannon, *Trumpets in the Morning* (Nashville: Broadman, 1969), p. 58.

our sermons. They gain interest, make vivid truth, and aid persuasion. Good illustrations will make clear the truth we are seeking to communicate, not call attention to themselves.

We are preaching to a visually minded generation. Psychologists claim we learn 85 percent through sight, 10 percent through hearing, 2 percent through touch, 1 1/2 percent through smell, and 1 1/2 percent through taste.[36] Assuming that is correct, the importance of illustrations in a sermon becomes apparent. We must make our sermons as lifelike as possible. Through the pictures illustrations produce in the minds of our hearers, we can make the abstract come to life. The mindset of today's modern congregations makes the effective use of illustrations a psychological necessity.

PURPOSES OF ILLUSTRATIONS

There are many purposes of sermon illustrations. The people can remember the truth you are communicating much better by means of a simple, to-the-point illustration. Good illustrations stir the emotions and move people to action. By means of an illustration you can create an awareness of need in your listeners. All of us have experienced the power of an illustration to hold the attention of our audience or to regain lagging attention. Illustrations are very helpful in building bridges to your listeners. Though they may not be especially interested in what you have to say, you can create interest and a favorable hearing by means of a well-presented illustration.

CHARACTERISTICS OF GOOD ILLUSTRATIONS

A good illustration clarifies the truth you are communicating. The unknown is interpreted by the known. If your illustration is a good one, it will help your people understand what you are trying to say.

Good illustrations assist in persuasion. Often a truth that may be resisted initially can gain a hearing by means of a simple illustration.

If the people can easily identify with the illustration, it is a good one. Too many preachers use illustrations from rural life when preaching to suburban congregations. Your people will completely miss the

36. Whitesell, p. 75.

point if they do not understand the particulars involved in the illustration.

Illustrations are effective when they pull the heartstrings of the people. I do not mean that the preacher must be melodramatic or sentimental. There is little value in telling a tearjerker just to "work up" the audience. But a good illustration will get to the hearts of the people. Most decisions are made in the heart, not in the head. Illustrations pry open the door of the heart.

An effective illustration will be colorful, not drab. Make use of the powers of simile and metaphor. Use the mechanism of parable. Flavor your illustrations with historical references, biographical references, and an intelligent awareness of the contemporary world.

Work hard to see that your illustrations actually illustrate the point. Make them fit. An illustration may be a very good one but fail to cast light upon the subject you wish to illustrate.

To be effective an illustration must touch the people where they live. Use illustrations taken from the real-life experiences of your people.

No illustration is good if it is inappropriate to the circumstances of the service or to the audience. Some illustrations are in poor taste. There is no place for crudeness or disrespect. I have been embarrassed on some occasions by the questionable nature of the illustrations preachers have used. Be sure every illustration you tell is in good taste.

Your illustration will be a good one if it is believable. An illustration that sounds far-fetched will immediately produce questions in the minds of your hearers. If you are making up an illustration, say so. If the story is imaginary, do not hesitate to tell your audience. Some fictitious illustrations can carry an impact if you wait until the end to tell the people it is fictitious. This is within the bounds of proper use. Just be sure you are absolutely honest in your use of illustrations.

THE LOCATION OF AN ILLUSTRATION

Placement of the illustration in the sermon is also an important matter. Determine where the illustration can carry the most force. Seek to avoid putting illustrations at the same place in each message.

You may want to begin your sermon with an illustration. You may want to amplify one of your main points with a good illustration just as soon as you state the point. Or you may want to wait until the end of the point to use your illustration.

I do not necessarily use an illustration for each truth I am trying to present. I do try to have a good illustration for each main point. A number of effective illustrations can greatly benefit the overall impact of your sermon.

SOURCES OF ILLUSTRATIONS

I have worked very hard to get illustrations for my sermons. When you preach to generally the same people week by week, year by year, the search for illustrations is a demanding assignment. The pastor cannot use the same illustrations over and over. Telling the same illustration several times can completely sap it of its vitality and appeal. The preacher must be constantly gathering fresh illustrations.

Where do you find good illustrations? Let me begin by telling you where not to find them. I have in my study a long row of sermon illustration books. I would be happy to sell every one of them to you, cheap. I have not found enough usable illustrations to make any of them worth the money I paid for them. The illustrations from such books are canned and outdated. I do not recommend you waste your money on them. If you insist on having an illustration book, one should suffice. Purchase *Encyclopedia of 7,700 Illustrations* by Paul Lee Tan (Rockville, Maryland: Assurance Publishers, 1979). I have used a few illustrations from this book.

There are much better sources of illustrations than illustration books. Personal reading in a wide range of topics will bring you across many illustrations suitable for your preaching. Personal experiences provide one of the best sources. You must be careful here. Too frequent reference to members of your family can annoy your people. But along the way you will have experiences that will aptly illustrate Bible truth. Do not hesitate to use these. The people can immediately identify with them.

Keep your eyes open all the time. You can glean illustrations from the world of nature. Helpful illustrations may be found in the experiences of others. In your reading of the daily newspaper, magazines, and other literature you can find good illustrations. Keep an illustration notebook. Placed in alphabetical order, arranged by subject, you can briefly note the illustrations you find by observation. I keep this notebook handy. I have many, many illustrations in my notebook that I have yet to use.

The Bible is a fruitful source of sermon illustrations. Use imagination in the Bible stories. Illustrate New Testament truths with Old Testament experiences. With a little touch of imagination you can effectively build these wonderful Bible stories into good illustrative material.

I have found the study of the original words of Scripture a good source of sermon illustrations. The Greek language is especially good at this point. Many Greek words are very picturesque. Whole illustrations can be found in the meaning of a Greek word. Dig these out in your word study during the exposition of the passage.

In listening to other preachers I very often find illustrations I can effectively use in my own sermons. Whenever I listen to another preacher I am careful to have a piece of paper and pen on hand.

Illustrations can actually be found anywhere. Be on the lookout for them. Work to increase your powers of observation. There is a sermon in every dewdrop and in every shaft of sunlight. If you search for them, you will find them.

CAUTIONS

The preacher should be mindful of certain cautions in his use of illustrations. First, be sure your illustrations are true. If you are making up an illustration, let it be known at the appropriate time. Do not tell something that happened to another person as if it happened to you. You could be very embarrassed by this. Second, be modest in your personal illustrations. Boastfulness will immediately cause your audience to be resentful and to resist what you are trying to say. Third, do not violate a confidence. Do not take matters told to you in privacy and use them as the basis of a sermon illustration. This can be very painful to the one whose confidence is broken.

EPIGRAMS AND WITTICISMS

Epigrams and witticisms are some of the oldest and most effective forms of expression. Even as early as 200 B.C. the Greeks were using epigrams that had brevity and unity of thought. Such writers as Sir Thomas More, Ben Johnson, George Bernard Shaw, and Oscar Wilde used them effectively. Epigrams can be used very effectively to point out men's failures, to prod men to action, to puncture pride, and to cause laughter.

An epigram is a bright or witty thought tersely or ingeniously expressed. A well-known definition of an epigram is:

> The qualities rare in a bee that we meet,
> In an epigram never should fail;
> The body should always be little and sweet,
> And the sting should be felt in its tail.

A witticism is a witty saying, sentence, or phrase.

Epigrams and witticisms may be sarcastic, satirical, or humorous. They may express criticism or praise. I have found them helpful in communicating a truth in a brief, pointed, catchy manner.

These expressions can enliven the message and sharpen its applications. They provide color to your message. Familiar truths may be stated in different ways. They can capture your meaning in a brief statement. For instance, "A faith that can't be tested, can't be trusted" says a great deal about faith in one brief sentence.

Epigrams can help your listeners better remember what you are trying to say. They give your listeners something to turn over in their minds. The truth is more understandable to them. Instead of saying, "Possessions can wreck a life," try saying, "It isn't wrong to have possessions; it is wrong for them to have you."

By the means of an epigram you can, in a few words, gently and in tasteful humor, destroy an unsound argument.

An epigram should not just be cute or funny. Use them only when they are pertinent to what you are saying.

Some are especially gifted in wording epigrams. I have not been so gifted, but that does not keep me from effectively using them. In recent years, as I run across epigrams and witticisms I file them in a notebook. I try to memorize many of them each week. I keep them on hand for ready reference. They can be found in many sources. Again, as in illustrations, listen for them in the sermons of others. Look for them in your regular reading. Herbert V. Prochnow's book

Speaker's Handbook of Epigrams and Witticisms (Grand Rapids: Baker, 1955) is a good source. E. C. McKenzie has a book entitled *Mac's Great Book of Quips and Quotes* (Grand Rapids: Baker, 1980). This is another good volume. Vance Havner's sermons are filled with epigrams and witticisms.

HUMOR

Another effective way of enhancing your message is the use of humor. I am aware that to use humor in the pulpit is considered by some to be making a joke of sacred things. In the early years of my ministry I used very little humor in the pulpit. On the one or two occasions I did, I was promptly reprimanded. This made me a bit wary for a time. We definitely do not want to joke or speak lightly of sacred things. Yet there is a legitimate use of humor.

We must not dehumanize ourselves or our listeners when we come to the house of God. Laughter is a part of life. Humor is natural to man. God has given us the ability to laugh. Evidently the Scripture places its approval upon appropriate expressions of humor. Proverbs 17:22 says, "A merry heart doeth good like a medicine." Proverbs 15:15 says, "He that is of a merry heart hath a continual feast." Why, then, must we strip ourselves of this God-given faculty? When we leave laughter and humor to the worldly comedians and amusement places of this world we are in a sad state. I am not appealing for an overly lighthearted or frivolous approach to preaching. I am merely saying that humor can be one tool in preparing effective sermons.

Let me make some suggestions about the use of humor in your sermons. Humor should add to your sermon, not detract. Make your humor appropriate to the subject at hand. Don't tell something funny just for the sake of telling it. Make the humor point toward what you are trying to communicate to the listeners.

Humor must be natural to you, if you are to use it effectively. Make your humor spontaneous. If you cannot do this, you probably would be best not to use humor. You can, however, cultivate a sense of humor. Do not fail to see the humor in your own life. To be able to laugh at yourself is a sign of maturity. Very often, the humorous things that happen to you can be effectively used in your sermons.

Many of God's great preachers have used humor effectively.

Warren Wiersbe (quite a humorist himself) writes about Dwight L. Moody and Gypsy Smith, "These men were not comedians; they were ambassadors—but joyful ambassadors. And because of their sanctified humor they were able to touch men for Christ. Not every preacher can do this, but those who can use humor should not bury their talent."[37]

Introducing

There is some difference of opinion concerning when the introduction of the sermon should be prepared. I suppose each preacher has his own preference. I leave the introduction to be done near the end of my preparation. I have always had a rather difficult time introducing something before I know what I want to introduce!

Regardless of when it is done, take time to prepare your introduction well. I have followed the practice of writing out in full my first sentence. A strong opening sentence prepares for a strong introduction. Someone has said, "Light your match on the first strike."[38] I use my first sentence to capture attention, and it also gives some indication of where I am heading.

PURPOSES OF THE INTRODUCTION

There are several purposes for the introduction. The introduction should gain interest and create attention. Failure to get the interest of the listeners in the beginning of the sermon forfeits one's opportunity to communicate. We cannot assume that those who sit in our audience are automatically interested in what we are going to say. We must create that interest. Songwriters use what they call a "hook" somewhere in the song to catch the listeners' attention. Why not place a "hook" in your introduction? Put something in the beginning of your sermon that will arouse the interest of your listeners. Haddon Robinson refers to a Russian proverb as counsel concerning the introduction: "It is the same with men as with donkeys; whoever would hold them fast must get a very good grip on their ears!"[39]

37. Warren Wiersbe, *Walking with the Giants* (Grand Rapids: Baker, 1976), p. 220.
38. Adams, p. 54.
39. Robinson, p. 160.

The first few minutes of your sermon you either have your listeners with you or you do not. In these early minutes the stage is set. The mood of the audience is determined. Since you are going to give yourself to the rigorous discipline of sermon preparation, be sure to gain a favorable hearing. Your purpose is to move the listeners to action, to help them make certain decisions on the basis of the sermon you have delivered. That cannot be accomplished if the listeners are not favorably inclined to your sermon. Someone has said there are three kinds of preachers: those you cannot listen to; those you can listen to; and those you must listen to. A good introduction will help you be the latter.

Any good introduction will prepare for what is to come. The central idea, or theme, of the Scripture passage from which you intend to preach has already been determined. You know what you want to say, but those who sit before you have no idea what you intend to say. In your introduction you should make sure your audience knows the theme of your sermon. Several brief, well-worded sentences of introduction should make that theme unmistakably clear.

Further, the introduction of your message is intended to move you quickly into the body of your sermon. We have already discussed the use of a key word as a means of holding your main points together. Using the key word in a full sentence, you can lead into your first main point. This sentence can provide a natural transition from the theme of the message into the body of the sermon. In the next section I will discuss more fully the conclusion and the invitation. The conclusion and the invitation should begin in the introduction. As you begin the message you should make clear to them where you are going. At the very outset of your sermon let them know what you expect of them. This should be a definite part of your introduction.

MARKS OF A GOOD INTRODUCTION

There are several marks of a good introduction. First, an introduction should be short. Do not spend too much time in the introduction. The preacher may be carried away as the sermon is begun. Avoid every word that is not absolutely necessary. Several years ago the distinguished senator and orator Albert J. Beveridge pointed out

"If you can't strike oil in three minutes, you should quit boring."[40] Spurgeon moved quickly through his introduction to the main body of the message. Spurgeon said you should plunge in at once over your head and ears. An elaborate, lengthy introduction may promise your listeners more than you are able to deliver. Robert G. Lee used to talk about preachers who built chicken-coop sermons on skyscraper foundations. Avoid this temptation. Be brief. An introduction is the porch, not the house. Make the introduction long enough to introduce the subject and no more.

Make use of variety in your introductions. When your listeners know you are going to begin each sermon the same way they will be prepared to give you only their inattention, not attention.

There are several ways to vary your introductions. Begin with a startling statement. This will get attention. Be sure, however, the statement is not so startling that everything thereafter is anticlimatic. Why not begin with an interesting quotation from a person well known to your listeners? This will very often get you started in an interesting and appealing way. An illustration may be used. This illustration should actually introduce what you are going to discuss in the message. A personal reference may sometimes be used as a method of introducing your sermon. Some life situation that directly relates to your message may be a good way to begin.

The contextual method is another way to introduce your sermon. The expository preacher faces a danger in this kind of introduction. Expository preachers have a tendency to gravitate to this method of introduction in their preaching. This can become very boring to those who regularly listen to expository sermons. On occasion, however, explaining the context can be a very good way to begin your message.

Another mark of a good introduction is that it turns quickly to the needs of the hearers. The introduction should arouse in them a sense of need. You cannot sell them something they do not know they need. Get to the needs of the people as quickly as possible. If you can touch genuine needs in your introduction, then deliver solutions to those needs throughout your message, you will be far along the road toward success in being an interesting preacher. Haddon

---

40. Judson Crandell, Gerald M. Phillips, and Joseph A. Wigley, *Speech: A Course in Fundamentals* (Glenview, Ill.: Scott Foresman, 1963), p. 169.

Robinson quotes a good statement about the importance of a good beginning: "Always grab the reader by the throat in the first paragraph, sink your thumbs into his windpipe in the second, and hold him against the wall until the tag line."[41]

UNDESIRABLE INTRODUCTIONS

There are several undesirable ways to introduce a sermon. Avoid the hem-and-haw introduction. In this introduction the preacher demonstrates he is not really sure what he is going to say. It is evident he has prepared neither the main body of the sermon nor the introduction. He is unclear in his thought, and his speech reflects his lack of clarity. He just "beats around the bush." An audience will notice this lack of preparation very quickly and will respond with hem-and-haw attention.

Never use an apologetic introduction. Do not apologize for your lack of preparation. Probably you will never prepare as well as you like for a sermon. There is always more work that could be done. But do not introduce your message by telling the people how poorly you have prepared or how little you know about the subject. They will know soon enough! Do not apologize for the nature of the subject you propose to discuss. If your sermon is expository, the subject is taken from the Bible. There is no need to apologize for any truth found in the Word of God. All truth has application to the hearts of the people.

The trite introduction should be avoided. Do not fill your introduction with meaningless, simple statements that do not point toward your subject. Make your introductory remarks weighty. You are seeking to arouse the attention of your listeners. You are asking them to give you their attention and thought for several minutes. You must give them enough substance in your introduction to merit this. If you are trite, they will not be impressed.

I have already cautioned against the pedantic introduction. A belabored, routine beginning will soon bore the listeners.

Avoid the misleading introduction. When the preacher proposes one subject and preaches on another, the people feel betrayed. Introduce your subject, then stick to it.

41. Robinson, p. 160.

Introductions should have a sense of tension. Create the awareness that your sermon will complete what you have begun in the
introduction. Indicate that the questions you have raised in the introduction will be answered in the main body of your message. The
needs you have identified in your introduction will be given Bible
solutions in the message. The introduction sets the pace for the entire
message.

The introduction also sets the mood for the sermon. Subjects
vary in mood. Some are happy and optimistic. Others are more serious
in nature. The introduction will quickly make known to the listeners
the mood of the sermon. You will want to match the mood of your
introduction with the subject. You do not want to begin in a frivolous
manner when you will be discussing a very serious subject. Set the
tone for your message at the beginning.

The people should be aware from the very beginning of the
sermon that you yourself are interested in the subject matter. Be
interested in what you are going to say. If *you* are interested, the
congregation is likely to be interested as well. Be sure to put yourself
into the introduction with your best thought and energy.

Adrian Rogers, pastor of Bellvue Baptist Church in Memphis,
Tennessee, has a useful formula for putting together a sermon introduction. Dr. Rogers thinks in terms of four words: Hey! You! Look!
Do! *Hey!* Get the attention of the listeners in the introduction. Catch
the essence of the sermon in a sentence. Gain their interest. *You!*
Indicate that the subject matter at hand applies to the listeners. This
is for you! I have something you need to hear. *Look!* Give some
information about the subject to come. Briefly show what will be
shared with them in more length and depth in the body of the message.
Do! Tell them what they are expected to do as result of hearing the
sermon. This is a very helpful formula in building an effective introduction.

Some preachers seem to care very little whether they are listened
to or not. Their messages seem to be soliloquies, intended for themselves alone. They might just as well be preaching to the trees and
stars. The preacher who is interested in communicating God's Word
to people will be most interested in securing their attention. The
majority of people who come to hear you preach really want to attend
to what you say. Be sure you do not stifle that desire in the opening

minutes of your sermon. Spurgeon said, "You must attract the fish to your hook, and if they do not come you should blame the fisherman and not the fish. Compel them to stand still awhile and hear what God, the Lord, would speak to their souls. The minister who recommended the old lady to take snuff in order to keep from dozing was very properly rebuked by her reply, 'If you would put more snuff into the sermon I would be awake enough!'"[42]

Concluding

The most neglected part of sermon preparation may well be the most important part. John Broadus, whose book *The Preparation and Delivery of Sermons* still stands as a classic in the field, says that rhetorically, psychologically, and spiritually the conclusion is next to the introduction as the most important part of the sermon. This is true because the conclusion ties together the different ideas and emphases of the sermon into one final thrust upon the minds and hearts of the listeners.

Whether or not it is the *most* important part of the sermon, careful attention must be given to the conclusion. Jay Adams says, "The conclusion is important as well as the introduction because it is important to have a good dessert as well as a good appetizer."

A sermon must come to some kind of ending. Your sermon must not just dribble away into nothingness. There must be a completion of the main theme of the sermon. Greek orators sometimes expressed their view of the conclusion by calling it "the final struggle which decides the conflict." For this reason the conclusion may indeed be the most significant part of your sermon. In the concluding moments the issues at hand are decided if they are indeed decided at all. During the conclusion you will bring to focus as clearly as you possibly can the timeless truths that your expository efforts have uncovered in the Scripture passage. Concluding time is the time to drive home your main theme. You are wrapping up what you have said. In a series of brief, crisp, telling sentences you are bringing the whole thrust of your message to bear upon your people.

Since the conclusion is such a necessary part of the sermon, why

---

42. Charles Haddon Spurgeon, *Lectures to My Students* (London: Marshall, Morgan and Scott, 1954), p. 128.

is it so often neglected in sermon preparation? There may be several reasons. The preacher may run out of time in his sermon preparation. The temptation is to tack on a brief, rather general summary to the message. A lack of time often causes the conclusion to suffer more than other areas of the sermon outline.

Many preachers today are faced with time limitations in the delivery of their messages. Because of radio or television deadlines the message must be concluded, whether the preacher is finished or not. This causes the preacher to jettison his message prematurely. If the preacher does not have time to get to a well-thought-out and prepared conclusion, why should he bother to prepare one?

Sometimes the conclusion is neglected because the other work of the sermon has not been properly done. The preacher will find it difficult to arrange a strong conclusion if there is no clear understanding of the unifying theme of the Scripture passage. If the main points have not logically developed this subject, there is really nowhere to go in concluding the message.

These reasons for neglect must be faced and overcome. The conclusion is too vital. The preacher must give much thought and preparation to building adequate conclusions to his sermons.

PRINCIPLES OF A GOOD CONCLUSION

Certain principles should guide you as you seek to prepare a good conclusion. First, the conclusion should reflect the main points. As we have previously indicated, repetition is an important method of amplifying truth. It may be the most effective method of emphasizing what you want to say. We have often been urged to tell them what we are going to tell them, tell them what we want to tell them, then tell them what we have told them. In your conclusion you will probably want to repeat certain phrases or words that summarize the main thrust of your sermon.

In addition, a good conclusion will be fitting to the sermon. I have heard some good conclusions that have had very little to do with the sermon they supposedly ended. If your sermon is one of encouragement, conclude with encouragement. If your sermon is a call to action, conclude with a ringing call to action.

Good conclusions will be characterized by clarity of thought and expression. There is no place for vagueness as you end a sermon. Your listeners must be able to understand without question what you are saying. A good practice in the early years of your ministry is to write out your conclusions. That will force you to clarify what you are saying.

Brevity is a good characteristic in conclusions as well as in introductions. Say what you want to say. Say it briefly. Say it pointedly, then be done.

Reserve some strength and energy for your conclusion. Do not so preach that you give out all you have before you reach the conclusion. Properly done, the conclusion is the climax of your message. You should build toward that. Broadus says, "It is a fault of some energetic speakers that they exhaust themselves before they reach the conclusion and come up panting and hoarse and with no banner but a moist handkerchief." Too often have I been guilty as charged! You will find that giving attention to the preparation of your conclusion will subconsciously enable you to reserve enough liveliness to carry your sermon to its proper ending.

A good conclusion sometimes will have the element of surprise. Properly done you can build your message to a climax, quickly move into the conclusion, wrap up the substance of your message in a few brief statements, and then stop. This can be very effective in the overall impact of your sermon. Normally you should not conclude by saying, "In conclusion," or, "Finally." If you are concluding, the people will not have to be told you are.

The preacher needs to develop a sense of timing in relation to the conclusion. Every preacher has experienced those occasions when he reached the climax of his sermon prematurely. At that point, the rest of the sermon was downhill. There have been those times in my own preaching ministry when I reached my climax but continued on. The sermon would have been much better if I had rapidly moved into my conclusion and brought the truth to bear with fire and intensity to the hearts of my hearers.

For the preacher to go beyond the best stopping point in his sermon is to subject his congregation to a decided letdown. There is an interesting story told about Mark Twain in this connection: "When the speaker had talked ten minutes I was so impressed I decided I would give every cent I had with me. After another ten minutes I concluded that I would throw into the treasure all the silver I had with me. Ten minutes later I decided I wouldn't give anything. At the end of the talk, still ten minutes later, as the contribution plate came around, I was so utterly exhausted by the arguments that I extracted two dollars for my own use."

Your conclusion will be effective if you make personal application. Direct your remarks to the people in your audience. What good reason is there to direct your message to those who are not there? They cannot hear. Those who do hear need something for themselves. You should make use of the second personal pronoun often in the conclusion. Appeal to individuals for a definite response. The conclusion should leave the people with a deep sense of personal responsibility. They should know beyond question what action on their part is called for.

FLAWS IN CONCLUSIONS

Effort should be made to avoid several common flaws in sermon conclusions. Avoid moralizing. To close your sermon by saying, "The moral of this sermon is . . ." is not effective. This indicates a lack of clear thinking. When the conclusion has not been carefully prepared one finds it easy to lapse into moralizing, which is normally too general and vague to be effective in closing a sermon.

As I have already indicated, you should stop your sermon when you are through. Do not press on after a good stopping point in the sermon. William Jennings Bryan's mother leveled with him after an evening's address with the painful words, "Will, you missed several good opportunities to sit down." Do not let your sermon ravel out like a ball of yarn at the end. When you are through, clip the loose ends, neatly tie them together, and leave your people with a well-thought-through sermon.

Likewise, do not stop before you are through. The message should be fully developed before you move into the conclusion. Your sermon must be carefully and properly organized if you are to avoid this problem.

Avoid the temptation to conclude by introducing new material. This is a common tendency among expository preachers. You are preaching through a book of the Bible. Next week you will begin in the Scripture where you conclude this week. There is the temptation to conclude what you are trying to say in this passage by taking a peek into the green fields of the next one. Guard against that. Your conclusion will be robbed of force and power. If you must say something about the sermon for next week, do so in the final remarks of the service. Don't preview next Sunday's message in your sermon conclusion.

Try a variety of conclusions. To conclude each week in the same manner robs you of the positive benefits of an unexpected ending for your sermon. When you always conclude in the same manner you let your listeners know you are concluding before you may want them to know. The element of surprise is completely destroyed. You may briefly summarize the essential elements of your sermon or close with an effective illustration. Try concluding with a telling quotation. End with a thought-provoking question. Do something different. Be unpredictable. Keep them guessing.

THE INVITATION

There is very little discussion in books on sermon preparation about the relationship of the conclusion to the invitation. Actually, very little is written on the invitation at all. That is unfortunate. The invitation is a key part of the sermon. We do not preach merely to hear ourselves talk. We do not preach simply to convey information. The congregation should not be led to have the attitude "Let us move to receive this sermon as information, and be dismissed." We are preaching for a response. Every sermon should be intended to change the lives of people in some definite way. All through the message we have been moving toward a purpose. We want something to happen in the hearts of those who hear our sermons. We are lawyers pleading our Lord's cause. We are calling for a verdict. The invitation is the time when the people make their response. The conclusion should include a definite invitation.

Every sermon I preach has what I call an "evangelistic twist." By this I mean that I turn the message, in conclusion, toward an appeal to the unsaved in the audience to receive Jesus Christ as personal Lord and Savior. Any expository sermon lends itself to this method. Bible preaching always points to evangelism. Bible preaching that does not ultimately call for the unsaved to receive Jesus Christ as personal Savior borders on heresy. Regardless of the Bible content of your message, the subject can be turned toward an evangelistic appeal.

There are many effective ways to give such an evangelistic twist to your sermon. If you are preaching on tithing, for instance, you can say something like this: "Perhaps there are many of you in the service who do not know Jesus as your personal Savior. What has tithing to do with you? Actually, it has nothing. Tithing is a spiritual matter between the believer and his Lord. If you do not know Jesus as your Savior, the Lord is not interested in your money. He is interested in you! He doesn't want your money. He wants you! I'm going to ask you today to give your heart and life to Him."

As you move into the invitation during the conclusion you need to become very personal and direct with your audience. An invitation may be given like this: "Dear Friend, I am going to invite you this very day to make the most important decision you have ever made in your life. I am going to invite you to receive Jesus Christ as your personal Lord and Savior. I do not believe you would be in the service today if in your heart of hearts you did not know you need Jesus Christ. In a few moments, as people pray for you, and as the choir sings a hymn of invitation, I am going to ask you to come forward publicly, expressing your desire to receive Jesus as Savior. We have counselors who are ready to explain to you from the Scriptures how you may know Jesus as your very own personal Savior. All the aisles lead to the front. As the choir begins to sing, on the first word of the first stanza I want you to leave where you are sitting [or standing], step into the nearest aisle, and come forward to receive Jesus. Won't you do it? Now is your time!"

Let me share with you some final suggestions made by Donald Demaray. End grandly and climactically. End genuinely. End fulfillingly. End emotionally. End knowingly. End assuredly. End persuasively.

5

Final Ingredients: Incubation, Composition, and Delivery

We come now to the final ingredients in a good expository sermon—a period of incubation, composing the sermon, and delivery.

I came upon the matter of incubation accidentally, but the experience was very real. I was unaware that incubation is part of a defined process in creativity. It is discussed little in most books on sermon preparation.

Drawing from my own experience in this area, I investigated what had been written by secular writers in the field of creativity. I was helped by what I found. The steps in the creative process are clearly defined and may be utilized in sermon preparation as well as in other fields of endeavor. I hope this section will trigger an interest on your part to put your subconscious mind to work on your sermons.

The section on sermon style is intended to assist you in putting your sermon together as effectively as possible. We discuss several ingredients of good sermon style and suggest ways to improve yours. Included is a discussion of the pros and cons of writing out your sermon in full. My approach may serve as a helpful compromise in this matter. The effectiveness of your sermon will be greatly increased as you polish and improve your sermon style.

The concluding section of this chapter is a discussion on preaching without notes. The prospect of doing so may be very frightening to you, but this section will give suggestions that will help. In this section I include a simple, easy-to-follow approach to preaching without sermon notes. Following these steps over a period of time will help you develop proficiency in extemporaneous preaching, which seems to be the best way to preach. I believe preaching without notes increases the effectiveness of your sermon.

How to Put Your Subconscious Mind to Work

Too little attention is given to the processes of creativity in sermon preparation. The preacher may do all the necessary spade work, organize the message well, yet still lack the creative spark that makes the sermon unique and effective. Creativity in sermon preparation can be better achieved through allowing time for the subconscious to work on the message.

In one sense a sermon is an act of creativity. After intensive sermon preparation the preacher brings forth from his mind and heart a new creation—an expository sermon. The sermon is born of the movement of the Holy Spirit upon the life and labors of the preacher. Even the preacher with minimum experience knows the wonderful burst of inspiration when all the pieces of the sermonic endeavor come together. Suddenly, the message comes with wholeness, unity, organization, and force. This is the creative experience of sermon preparation.

Thus far in our study we have been primarily concerned with the steps in the sermon preparation process. But the preacher can become too conscious of the mechanics. He can actually over-prepare. He risks "studying himself stupid." The preacher can get his wings so heavy that he cannot fly. All of us have faced those times when we cannot seem to get the sermon to "come together." We find ourselves mentally paralyzed. The solution to such a dilemma is found in allowing sufficient time for the subconscious mind to work on the sermon.

SUBCONSCIOUS INCUBATION

There is tremendous help in what I call subconscious incubation. Some writers refer to this as maturation. We touched briefly upon this subject in the discussion concerning reading the passage of Scripture. John Stott says, "Read the text. Reread it, reread it, and read it again. Probe your text like a bee with a spring blossom, or like a hummingbird probing a flower for nectar."[1] This is certainly a part of allowing the subconscious mind to focus itself upon the passage. But the process of incubation in sermon preparation is much more extensive.

Several interesting studies on incubation and the process of creativity have been made. One of the most interesting is in Rollo May's book *The Courage to Create*. May defines creativity as the process of making or bringing into being. In his discussion he points out that we use many different expressions that indicate what creativity is. Such expressions as "a thought pops up," or "an idea comes from the blue," or "it suddenly hit me" all indicate different ways of picturing the experience of creativity. Somewhere beneath the level of conscious awareness, ideas break through into our experience.

May describes the phenomenon: "Often when one works at a hard question, nothing good is accomplished at the first attack. Then one takes a rest, longer or shorter, and sits down anew to the work. During the first half hour, as before, nothing is found, and then all of a sudden the decisive idea presents itself to the mind. It might be said that the conscious work has been more fruitful because it has been interrupted and the rest has given back to the mind its force and freshness."[2]

Almost every person involved in some kind of creative endeavor has experienced this sudden burst of illumination or insight. May explains how the process has worked in his own experience: "I may have worked at my desk morning after morning trying to find a way to express some important idea. When my insight suddenly breaks through—which may happen when I am chopping wood in the afternoon—I experience a strange lightness in my step as though a great load were taken off my shoulders, a sense of joy on a deeper level that continues without any relation whatever to the mundane tasks that I may be performing at the time."[3]

Very often some of the most significant breakthroughs have taken place in this manner. Individuals have labored earnestly trying to solve a particular problem and have been unable to do so. Then suddenly and unexpectedly, in a moment when they were not consciously think-

1. John R.W. Stott, *Between Two Worlds* (Grand Rapids: Eerdmans, 1982), p. 220.
2. Rollo May, *The Courage to Create* (New York: Bantam, 1975), p. 70.
3. Ibid., p. 147.

ing about the problem, the answer came. Martyn Lloyd-Jones relates the story of a great mathematician who was working on a mathematical problem. He had been working on the problem for months, but the solution evaded him. He was convinced a solution could be found but was unable to find it. After many months of mental logjam he felt the need to stay for a few days at a small seaside village. Perhaps the change of air would help him. He took his work with him, thinking he might be able to do some additional work at the seaside. He worked for a time, but still with no solution to the problem. In his frustration he decided to pay a visit to some of his colleagues in Paris. Perhaps they could give him assistance. He took a little bus from the village to a nearby town where he would change to a larger bus. As he stepped off onto the platform, suddenly the solution to his mathematical problem appeared before him plainly. It had come to him as out of the blue.[4]

This has happened to me many, many times. The experience is a strange, mysterious, yet greatly exhilarating one. There have been times I found myself in a mental tangle. I knew the message could be organized much better, but I could not find how to do it. On occasion, the points that would make the sermon clear have eluded me. I sensed they were there, but I could not seem to dig them out of the passage. Then, at an odd moment, everything came together. I saw the truth of the passage clearly. The main points suddenly came in clear, concise, logical order. This has happened to me under every imaginable circumstance. I have had the experience while driving to work. In the middle of the night I have been awakened with a sudden burst of insight. I have even had these moments of inspiration in the shower! What took place? Somehow my subconscious mind worked on the sermon, brought it all together, resolved the problems, and presented the solution as a much-needed gift to my conscious mind.

PHASES IN THE CREATIVE PROCESS

Horace Rahskoph has presented a good explanation of the phases in the process of creativity. He says there are four. Phase one Rahs-

4. D. Martyn Lloyd-Jones, *Preaching and Preachers* (Grand Rapids: Zondervan, 1971), pp. 210-11.

koph calls *preparation.* This is a time of sustained preliminary labor. During this phase you expose yourself to the widest possible range of information about the subject. All relevant facts about the subject at hand are assembled, digested, organized, and comprehended. Every bit of information from one's past experience, reading, insight, and observation is considered. During this phase, one must be especially receptive to new, unique ideas. A conscious effort must be made to avoid putting facts in old, comfortable classifications. Effort must be made to seek new relationships and categories of thought.

The second phase Rahskoph calls *incubation.* This is time given to germination and maturing of the main ideas. The previous preparation and the intensive labor involved may have led to a kind of mental indigestion. A time of rest or recreation is needed. This gives the mind time to digest and assimilate the information one has gathered. This time of incubation may involve a change of activity or a complete rest. The length of this time will vary. Whatever the length of time, the unconscious mind is reworking and reorganizing the gathered information. This gives the unconscious mind the opportunity to perceive on its own. This rest or change of activity will release the person from intensive effort and allow the creative impulse free rein to express itself. Eventually, new ideas will emerge. Periods of preparation and incubation may recur in alternation as successive stages of work and rest.

Phase three is *illumination.* This is the moment of insight. Such a moment may come at the time of the break between the periods of preparation and incubation. The idea emerges, sometimes with apparent suddenness. The idea may come unexpectedly, without effort, often during moments of relaxation. This dynamic process comes out of periods of study, matures in the hidden subjective levels of thought| and springs into life with a startling suddenness. There very often comes with this moment of illumination a deep sense of satisfaction and confidence.

Frequently this new insight may come against what has been tenaciously held to in one's previous perceptions. There is often a brevity and conciseness of insight that has previously been unattainable. This burst of illumination comes after much hard work has been done on the subject in prior efforts.

Rahskoph's fourth phase is *verification.* The creative idea must then be developed and elaborated in terms of the surrounding context. The inspired concept must now be checked with the available facts that have been brought forth in the previous period of preparation. This enables one to verify and authenticate the accuracy of the creative idea.[5]

CREATIVITY AND SERMON PREPARATION

Rahskoph's phases in the process of creativity can readily be applied to the discipline of sermon preparation. Subconscious incubation is a definite step in the process that leads to an expository sermon. The preacher must do thorough preparation. The steps involved in the exposition of a passage must be carried out. Time must also be spent in the process of organizing the Scripture passage. But there must also be incubation time if the sermon is to become all the preacher wants it to be. The subconscious mind must be given the opportunity to work on the content that has been assembled.

As the preacher meditates on his Scripture passage he is preparing the way for the creative process. The preacher can meditate upon his sermon at many times when he is not in his study. He can do relaxed thinking about his passage under many different circumstances. He can do this as he walks, jogs, or drives. From time to time during the preparation of a message I spend several minutes allowing my mind to freely travel the many roads of the passage. I try to avoid familiar roads upon which I have previously traveled. I look for different, out-of-the-ordinary entrances into the Scripture portion. I am often amazed at what these brief times of meditation can do.

Putting the imagination to work on the Scripture passage can also be a positive step toward creativity. Imagination is the capacity of the mind to receive a bombardment of ideas, impulses, and other kinds of psychic phenomena that well up from the subconscious mind. Imagination provides the capacity to "dream dreams and see visions."[6] You will be amazed at the new insights and concepts that will emerge from the subconscious if you will allow your imagination time to work on your Scripture passage.

5. Horace G. Rahskoph, *Basic Speech Improvement* (New York: Harper and Row, 1965), pp. 181-83.
6. May, p. 144.

There must be, in addition to brief snatches of meditation time, more extended periods of time in order for incubation to take place. In recent years I have found one helpful way to allow time for the creative process to work. I begin my sermon preparation on Monday morning. I plan to complete it at the end of my Friday morning study time. A very useful procedure for me is to use my Thursday morning for alternate study. I get the basic work done on my message in the Monday through Wednesday study times. On Thursday I set aside my sermon preparation for the coming Sunday. My attention is turned to outside reading, writing projects, and a variety of other study activities. I do not consciously give myself to the study of my sermons on that day. Later on in the afternoon or at night, in a different place, under a different set of circumstances, I look again at my sermon. Many times I am thrilled to see how much clearer the passage is after some time away from it. Very often, the sermon outline arranges itself in a much more logical, clear manner. The sermon thesis appears in sharper focus than previously.

The moment of illumination in your sermon preparation may come during that day away from your preparation. The creative moment may come during a time of recreation. You may even be attending a meeting. The time or place makes no difference. Just keep a pen and some paper on hand. When the creative moment comes, be sure to get down what you receive. My suggestions may not work for you. Find out what will, but give some time to allowing your subconscious to work on your sermon.

THE HOLY SPIRIT AND CREATIVITY

The concept of incubation may be another way of expressing the role the Holy Spirit plays in sermon preparation. All through the preparation of an expository sermon the preacher must keenly feel his dependence upon the Holy Spirit. The One who inspired the Scriptures must also give the one who would preach them understanding and insight into their meaning. The Holy Spirit must place in the hands of the preacher the keys that actually unlock their meaning and provide their application. Perhaps those times when we allow the subconscious mind to work on the sermon are those occasions when we have opened our lives to the direction of the Holy Spirit in a new and meaningful way. For this reason the expository preacher must saturate his sermon preparation with prayer. Do as much of your sermon preparation as you can on your knees. Someone has said, "Work without prayer is atheism; but prayer without work is presumption."

When the creative moment has come, quickly verify its accuracy in relation to the facts you have found in your expository investigation. Arrange your outline accordingly. Restate your unifying theme, if necessary. The sermon now is more than just a set of organized facts. The message breathes with new, fresh life. You are ready to compose your sermon.

Let me close this section with a very helpful illustration from the preaching career of D. Martyn Lloyd-Jones.

> I well remember how on one occasion I was struggling with a text and had spent the whole morning on it, but simply could not get it in shape. My wife then called me to lunch. At that time there was a man named Christopher Stone who had a weekly radio program of new gramophone records. We used to enjoy listening to that program. Listening to the music I was pleased and deeply moved. Immediately the problem I had been struggling with for hours throughout the morning was entirely resolved. Everything fell into place at once—order, divisions, shape, everything. The moment the record finished I rushed to my study and put it down on paper as quickly as I could, trusting that I had not forgotten or missed anything. That singing and that music provided the release I needed from my mental tangle and stalemate.[7]

There is much to be learned about this neglected area of sermon preparation. I recommend that you learn as much about the process of creativity as you can. Your ability to prepare expository sermons will be greatly benefited. I covet for you the experience, over and over again, of being involved with the Lord in bringing to birth a fresh message for the people.

How to Compose an Expository Sermon

We have done our work of exposition. We have organized our sermon, following the steps that lead to good organization. Sufficient

---

7. Lloyd-Jones, p. 212.

opportunity has been given to allow the creative process to occur. With the raw materials necessary to a sermon and the spark of inspiration the Holy Spirit has provided now in our possession, we are ready to compose an expository sermon.

I want to share with you the procedure I follow. I work from half sheets of paper. My sermon material is organized around each main point, which is placed on a separate piece of paper. If I have three main points, I use three half sheets of paper. On these sheets of paper I place the results of my sermon preparation. Under the appropriate points and subpoints I arrange every item of material I have gathered during the process of my expository work. Thoughts that have come to me about the passage are placed appropriately. I add the results of word study, parallel passages, and commentary information. I try to internalize ideas I read from others.

After these notations have been placed on paper, they must be composed in some form. The thoughts and truths of your sermon must become certain specific words either now or at the moment of delivery. My practice has been to take the sermon material I have gathered and the completed outline I have organized, then put them into some kind of complete form. At this point some preachers stop short in the matter of sermon preparation. Using only the bare skeleton of an outline, they have no specific arrangement and composition to their material. But that is unwise. A sermon must be put into particular words that convey its ideas. To fail to do this is to face the danger of being indefinite, abstract, and wordy. The sermon may have good content but will be lacking in a style that can be most effective in getting the passage from the printed page into the hearts of the hearers. The preacher must give careful attention to the matter of composing the sermon in an effective style.

SERMON STYLE

All of us do have a style, whether good or bad. Your style is your choice of words to convey the truths of your sermon. The choice of words the preacher makes for the delivery of his sermon can render the sermon powerfully effective or miserably inept.

Broadus, in speaking of style, says: "Style is the glitter and polish of the warrior's sword, but is also its keen edge. It can render mediocrity acceptable and even attractive, and power more powerful still. It can make error seductive, while truth may lie unnoticed for want of its aid. Shall religious teachers neglect so powerful a means of usefulness?"[8] The obvious value of good sermon style should make it a matter of the most careful attention on the part of the expository preacher.

MARKS OF POOR STYLE

There are several marks of a poor style. Verbosity is one of the most common. Too many words to express one's thoughts can hinder the desired effect and actually produce weariness on the part of the listeners. The preacher should work to eliminate as much as possible every unnecessary word.

Lack of clarity is also a mark of poor style. Sentences that are too long, ideas that are poorly arranged, phrases that are too complicated all cloud the truths you intend to convey to your listeners.

Another mark of poor sermon style is circumlocution. This defect is almost always fatal. The words promise the point but never seem to arrive. This is the error of saying many words but never really saying what you intend to say. As was said of one preacher with this problem, "If our dear brother had anything to say, he could certainly say it!"

Lack of dramatic quality is a mark of poor sermon style. The words have no alluring quality; they do not arouse a sense of interest and expectancy.

Absence of flow and rhythm greatly hinder good sermon style. The jerky sentence, the clumsy phrase, the hesitant expression are all indicative of poor sermon style. Closely akin to the absence of rhythm is the prominence of rhythm. This is monotony. The sentences are all the same. The movement is always predictable. There is no variety in what the preacher says and in the way he says it.

INGREDIENTS OF GOOD STYLE

In the composition of your sermon you should strive to achieve several important ingredients. First, you should seek to be clear in

---

8. John A. Broadus, *The Preparation and Delivery of Sermons* (New York: Harper, 1926), p. 225.

what you say. If the people do not know what you are saying, why preach at all? All technical, theological terminology should be rigorously removed. The sermon must be spoken in words the people know. Haddon Robinson illustrates my point quite well: "As one bewildered church-goer expressed it, 'the trouble is that God is like the minister; we don't see him during the week and we don't understand him on Sunday.'"[9] I have always considered myself supremely complimented when I am told the little children can understand what I say. I have taken the approach that, if I put the cookies on the bottom shelf, the rabbits can eat them and so can the giraffes.

Several matters should be kept in mind to achieve clarity of style. First, the choice of terms is very important. Use words that are clear. You would be wise to listen carefully to the advertisements on radio and television. Read the ads in magazines and the words on billboards. Advertisers are interested in selling a product. They want to get their message to the people as clearly as possible. The preacher should learn from them. This does not mean he should resort to slang to preach God's Word. Rather, the preacher will attempt to use clear words. Second, construct your sentences simply. They should be short. Make them as uncomplicated as possible.

A sermon can be more effective if there is vividness in style. Make your words come alive. The people should see what you say. They will be able to remember what you have said much longer if your words paint pictures for them. Vivid language conjures images in the minds of your people. The use of concrete words will make your sermon more vivid. Don't say, "A small Southern town. . . ." Say, "Homersville, Georgia." Don't say, "The beggar walked down the street." Say, "The beggar stumbled down the street."

There are several key features of vividness. Words are more vivid when they carry a feeling of suspense. They arouse a feeling of uncertainty. Sometime try presenting arguments on the other side of your sermon as though they were your own. This will immediately make your words come to life. Climax is another way to increase vividness. Try arranging your thoughts in order of their ascending power. This eases mental fatigue and provides a method of measuring your final conclusions. Words are more vivid when they are energetic.

9. Haddon W. Robinson, *Biblical Preaching* (Grand Rapids: Baker, 1980), p. 72.

Do not mistake energy for fury. Simple, specific words, phrased effectively, will provide tremendous energy. Give your statements a sense of movement. Let your words indicate you are going somewhere.

Your sermon style will be more effective if you use simple words. When you must use big words, be sure to explain them. Complicated words may impress a few but will confuse the majority. A traveler, driving a horse and carriage, arrived at a hotel and gave the following instructions to the young attendant who met him: "Extricate the quadruped from the vehicle, as he has toiled strenuously ever since the orb of day appeared on the eastern horizon this morning. Extend to him a munificent supply of nutritious victuals." The poor, bewildered young man ran to the hotel, told his master there was a man outside speaking Greek. "Will you please come and interpret for me?" he said. It would have been so much better if the traveler had simply said: "Take this horse to the stable; he has been working hard all day. Give him plenty to eat."[10] The words of a sermon should be simple, rather than artificial and impressive.

Good sermon style will make use of specific words. The correct choice of a word can make the difference in conveying your thought. Mark Twain said that the difference between the right word and the nearly right one is the difference between lightning and lightning bug.

Yet another evidence of good sermon style is freshness of expression. Be constantly on the lookout for new ways to say what you want to say. A catchy literary device may help you give what you are going to say a new, interesting twist. One time in preaching on the Bible word *glory,* I discovered the Bible teaches the glory of God is behind, above, before, within the believer. In trying to say this in a fresh way, I thought of the familiar tune "Old McDonald Had a Farm." So I said, "For the believer there is glory everywhere. There is glory here, glory there; here a glory, there a glory, everywhere a glory, glory." I said what I wanted to say in a fresh, new way.

Your sermon style should strive for some degree of beauty. In many ways a sermon, properly composed, is a work of art. Touches of beauty throughout can make it much more appealing to those who

---

10. George Henderson, *Lectures to Young Preachers* (Edinburgh: B. McCall Barbour, 1961), p. 78.

listen. Tolstoy once said, "What is art? . . . Once, when correcting a pupil's study Bruloff [a Russian artist] just touched it in a few places and the poor, dead study immediately became animated. 'Why you only touched it a wee bit, and it is quite another thing!' said one of the pupils. 'Art begins where the wee bit begins,' replied Bruloff, indicating by these words what is most characteristic of art. The teaching of the school stops where the wee bit begins—consequently where art begins."[11]

Give your sermon a touch of art. Use some parallelism in its phrasing. This will give a sense of grace and balance to your style. Use the repetition of an idea for emphasis and effect. Often a repeated phrase packs a real punch. Martin Luther King delivered a message that has become world famous. The message was built around the repetition of the phrase "I have a dream." Some time ago I preached an Easter message on the resurrection. I built the entire message around a single statement, "I'm going to live forever." Throughout the sermon I repeated this statement. Throughout the message I built upon this statement. The message built to a tremendous climax.

Strive to be very personal in your sermon style. Address your listeners personally. Use the personal pronoun *you* often. This will make your sermon much more appealing to those who listen.

WAYS TO ENHANCE SERMON STYLE

Do not suppose you will immediately begin to compose sermons that are gems of effective style. There are preachers who are unusually gifted in composing sermons, but regardless of your gifts in this area, you can improve. Pay attention to your way of speaking. Are your sentences too long and involved? Are your words specific and clear? When you speak, is there a simplicity and vividness about what you say? Be always working to improve the way you say things.

Spend time studying the style of others. Read books by good writers. Watch their use of language. Listen to effective preachers. Notice how they use language. Give attention to the kinds of words they use.

The preacher who would be more effective in his sermon style

11. H.A. Overstreet, *Influencing Human Behavior* (New York: Norton, 1925), p. 92.

must spend time working on his writing and speaking. If you do write, go over what you have written, giving careful attention to the qualities of good style. Listen to your taped sermons. Check your sentence structure. Listen to the words you use.

This brings us to a consideration of the question. Should you write out your sermon in full? Some preachers do. Probably most do not. The average preacher preaches so many sermons in a week's time he finds it difficult to write each of them in full. I will not be dogmatic at this point. Each preacher is different. Some of the greatest preachers in the past and in the present have written their sermons, and others have not.

The young preacher might do well to write out at least one sermon per week. This is good discipline in the early years of one's ministry. Writing does enable you to work on ways to improve your style. It serves to clarify one's thinking and assists in testing the sermon for its practical application to the people. There seems to be no question but that writing out a sermon will improve a preacher's style.

Some preachers take their sermon notes and dictate them. A secretary then types them out in full. This enables the preacher to talk out his message in full.

My approach has been to write out a full sentence sermon outline. Within this outline I may write certain sections in full. An illustration is normally written out in full. I work carefully on ways of saying certain things I want to say. These sentences and phrases are normally written out in full. Sometimes I will write a full introduction and conclusion. This enables me to work specifically on crucial sections of the sermon. Writing only part of the message avoids becoming too concerned about the exact wording of the sermon at the moment of delivery. This also avoids the danger of over-preparation. The sermon can be so overdone that it becomes a means within itself. In the next section we will discuss the matter of sermon delivery. There we will see that it may not be necessary to write out the sermon in full in order to deliver it effectively. Actually, the very opposite may be true.

The emphasis here is merely that a sermon is more than a disjointed compilation of Bible facts and practical applications. There should be some kind of sermon composition that utilizes the basic ingredients of effective style.

How to Preach Without Notes

No sermon, however effectively prepared, will accomplish the intended purpose unless it is delivered well. Thus far in our discussion of sermon preparation we have been talking primarily about manufacturing the product. Now we turn our attention to marketing. The best product is of little use if it cannot be brought effectively and quickly to the consumer.

Most of the preparation preachers have received in formal training has been lacking in this area. To get the content of an expository sermon is relatively simple. To adequately deliver that content is not so simple.

The biggest complaint I hear from the people about their pastor is that he uses a manuscript or notes. Constant looking down at his paper hinders the effectiveness of his delivery. Of course, some men can use a manuscript or sermon notes quite well. They have developed techniques that enable them to rely upon some form of written sermon help without making it noticeable. Most cannot.

In the beginning months of my ministry I used extensive sermon notes in the pulpit. Many, many pages of notes lay before me as I preached my sermons. Perhaps you have heard about the preacher whose sermon notes were blown by a gust of wind from the pulpit through the window. A cow came along, ate them—and went dry! Probably my sermon notes fell into that category. An older preacher in my congregation tactfully suggested I might do better to learn to preach without reliance upon notes. I had developed the unfortunate habit of looking up and down from my notes to the people. The effect was something like a chicken drinking water. Since I was eighteen years old at the time, my preacher friend suggested that my youth would make it possible for me to develop habits of preparation and study that would free me from the use of notes in the pulpit. His advice was taken. Never have I regretted developing the method of note-free preaching.

METHODS OF SERMON DELIVERY

There are four basic ways to deliver a message. One is *manuscript delivery*. The preacher reads the manuscript word for word. In this method the sermon has been written out in full. The great advantage of this method is that you can give careful attention to the choice of your words and the beauty of the language. Also, any anxiety about the possibility of forgetting your sermon is remedied. The disadvantages of this method are obvious. A sermon that is read most often will sound read. Rare is the preacher who can read so well that the sermon seems to be coming from his heart as well as from his head. Reading a manuscript loses the sense of live communication. There is a strong tendency to monotony.

The second method of sermon delivery is *preaching from memory*. In this method the sermon is written out in full, committed to memory, then delivered without any reference to manuscript or notes. The dangers of this particular method are so great there is little to commend it. The memorized sermon too often sounds memorized. The preacher who can deliver a full sermon from memory without creating the impression that he is giving it from memory is the exception, not the rule. There is always the danger of lapses in memory as well. To attempt to deliver an entire sermon depending only upon one's powers of memory is a feat most preachers would hesitate to attempt.

A third method of sermon delivery is the *impromptu*. Using this method the preacher speaks "off the cuff" or "from the top of his head." No prior preparation is made. He stands and says what comes to his mind at the moment of delivery. The occasions when such a method would be used are rare. This method is completely contrary to everything we have discussed in this book. No effective expository sermon can be delivered this way. There may be times when the preacher is called upon suddenly to deliver a message. In those times, however, whatever may be the Scripture the preacher chooses to use, he will draw upon previous preparation. This method has nothing to commend it to the serious preacher of God's Word.

The *extemporaneous* method is the fourth kind of delivery. This method is based upon careful, thorough preparation. In the study the preacher prepares as carefully as he possibly can, but waits for the moment of actual delivery to form his ideas into actual words. Only the actual wording of the sermon is left to the moment of delivery. The logical flow of ideas is clearly established. The sequence of ideas will be the same even though the choice of the particular words may vary. This method is probably the most commonly used among expository preachers.

Certain disadvantages of the extemporaneous approach to sermon delivery must be avoided. If the preacher is not careful, he will find himself using over and over the same words, phrases, and terminology. To speak extemporaneously one also faces the danger of rambling. Further, should the preacher be especially gifted in this method of speaking he may tend to abuse his ability. When the preacher relies too heavily upon his gifts in extemporaneous speaking he may tend to relax his habits of study. When this happens the extemporaneously delivered sermon becomes terribly bad. Done poorly, extemporaneous preaching can bring discredit to the expository method of sermon preparation.

ADVANTAGES OF EXTEMPORANEOUS DELIVERY

Several advantages can be cited for extemporaneous speaking. Great freshness in expression is possible. When the words are reserved for the moment of delivery the preacher may have in his full control all the variable factors in a good speaking situation. In this connection Broadus says: "If, full of his theme and impressed with its importance, he (the preacher) presently secures the interested and sympathizing attention of even a few good listeners, and the fire of his eyes comes reflected back from theirs, till electric flashes pass to and fro between them and his very soul glows and flames—he cannot fail sometimes to strike out thoughts more splendid and more precious than ever visit his mind in solitary musing."[12]

Further, extemporaneous preaching allows the preacher to observe how his message is being received. As he continues through the message he may change the ways of expression, as well as the manner of his delivery, according to response of the audience. In this manner the sermon may be delivered utilizing fully the voice, the eye, the body, and every factor of speaking just as they are intended to be used.

To speak extemporaneously is tremendously profitable in helping the preacher develop freedom and spontaneity of expression. As the

12. Broadus, p. 327.

preacher develops this faculty of ready expression he will learn to voice new thoughts that come to him as he delivers his sermon. This offers tremendous spontaneity to his sermon proclamation.

Practice in delivering sermons by means of the extemporaneous method helps develop what Jay Adams calls full fluency. This is the ability to choose words that are right orally and psychologically at high speed and arrange them in clear and effective speech.[13]

Adams also mentions another advantage of extemporaneous preaching: the jelling factor. Adams says that jelling is the result of good preparation. As the preacher preaches, careful preparation and previous extensive thought come together during the delivery of the sermon.[14]

THE METHOD OF GREAT PREACHERS

Many of the great preachers in the Christian faith have used the extemporaneous method. As Blackwood points out, this was the method of Alexander Maclaren. Blackwood says that Maclaren prepared for each sermon very carefully. Actually he prepared more carefully than if he were planning to read the message or speak it from memory. Then he allowed the words to well up from his heart at the moment of delivery.[15] As Blackwood also cites, this was the method of G. Campbell Morgan, known as the prince of expositors. Morgan believed that manuscript or notes would interfere with the eye contact characteristic of animated conversation.[16]

Perhaps a composite method may utilize the advantages of several different kinds of sermon delivery. Why not carefully prepare, even to the point of writing out, certain sections of your sermon? Then, read over what you have written. Keep in mind that there is a great difference between oral and written language. Remember that written language is intended for the eye. Oral language is meant for the ear. So, as you read over your manuscript or outline notes, try speaking what you have in your printed material. Then leave your manuscript

13. Jay Adams, *Pulpit Speech* (Phillipsburg, N.J.: Presbyterian and Reformed, 1971), p. 116.
14. Ibid., p. 114.
15. Andrew Blackwood, *Preaching from the Bible* (New York: Abingdon, 1941), p. 48.
16. Andrew Blackwood, *Expository Preaching for Today* (Grand Rapids: Baker, 1943), p. 157.

or notes behind and trust your memory. This method has all the advantages of the written sermon without the disadvantage of trying to read a manuscript in the pulpit. This method has careful preparation, yet retains the dynamics of free delivery.

I am going to suggest a basic pattern to follow to enable you to preach without notes. I am indebted to Charles W. Koller's excellent work for the three-step procedure I now suggest. To preach without notes involves three steps.

1. _Organization._ First, there must good organization. Your sermon must be carefully prepared. The sermon must have clear, concise main points. These points must be as simple as possible. Keep them to an absolute minimum. Use a good form of outlining. Make use of the visual aids in outlining I suggested in the chapter on outlining. If your sermon is organized properly, you are well on the way to note-free delivery.

2. _Memorization._ A certain amount of memorization is necessary. Your main points must be memorized. If you have drawn them from the Scripture passage itself, mere reference to the passage will help you to remember them. Certain key phrases might need to be memorized. Perhaps a better word than memorize would be _familiarize._ If you memorize these phrases or key expressions, your eyes may be lackluster and focus inward as you try to remember the words.[17] Try reading your notes aloud. Do this a number of times. Think about what you are saying as you say it aloud. Put your notes aside and try to recreate the basic sections of your message. Overlearn your material. Depend on logical memory rather than verbal memory.

3. _Saturation._ The third step to note-free preaching is saturation. Immerse yourself in your sermon. Get yourself into the sermon—get the sermon into you. Let the sermon become a part of your very being. Stamp the essentials of your message upon your consciousness so deeply that you will not fail to recall its essentials. As the time approaches for the delivery of the sermon go over it again and again. On Saturday night go over your sermon before going to bed. Make this the last thing you do. This will assist in putting the subconscious mind to work on the message.

When the time comes to deliver the message, rely upon the Lord

17. Dorothy Sarnoff, _Speech Can Change Your Life_ (New York: Dell, 1970), p. 203.

to help you. Prayer has been a vital part of your preparation all along the way. Now you are ready to share with the people what God has revealed to you from His Word and what has been indelibly stamped upon your mind and heart.

But what if you forget? Does the preacher who preaches without notes not sometimes forget? The answer is yes. There are times when I leave out something I thought to be very important. But if the impression of what I wanted to say was so weak I could not remember, probably it is best that the material be left out of the sermon. In a positive vein, often thoughts I had not intended to include come during the delivery of the message. This has become a very exciting part of my preaching ministry. I just prepare as if it all depends upon me, then stand to preach as if it all depends upon the Lord.

Each man will have to determine for himself what is the best method of sermon proclamation. The conviction I hold concerning note-free preaching is based upon my own years of experience. There are many advantages to note-free preaching. Do not allow your fears to hinder you from at least giving the method a try.

Conclusion

These are exciting days to be a preacher. Almost daily new and thrilling concepts are emerging in the field of sermon preparation. Today's preacher has in his hands tools and techniques that will enable him to preach the Word of God more effectively than ever before. My prayer is that this volume will be a positive contribution.

In one sense sermon preparation is a science. Much of the substance of this book has approached sermonic preparation from this dimension. We may learn from the experts in the field of homiletics. Good books on sermon preparation can improve our techniques of preparation. For this reason may I encourage you to stay abreast with what is being written in the field of homiletics. Learn the basics of good sermon preparation. Never minimize the value of techniques that make for good sermon preparation. Is the fire of heaven burning in your soul? Learning the techniques of sermon preparation will help you channel that fire into more effective means of reaching people with God's eternal Word.

In another sense, however, sermon preparation is an art. Not only must we learn from the homiletics professor, we must also learn from the effective preacher. The man who is preaching can be a role model for us. Listen to those who know how to preach. Preaching must not only be taught; it must be caught. Get acquainted with some good preachers. Talk with them about preaching. Learn from them methods that have made them effective.

I have approached this book on sermon preparation with one primary qualification. I write from the perspective of one who is actually involved in the week-to-week discipline of sermon preparation. I face the same time pressures you do. I encounter the tensions between what the "experts in the field" say to do and what actually works in my weekly preparation. For this reason, the book should have a down-to-earth flavor. If the book will help you get hold of some practical techniques for your own sermon preparation, I will be richly rewarded.

Preparing effective expository sermons can be a most frustrating work. Weekly my own heart is overwhelmed with a sense of inadequacy. Who among us can do justice to our responsibility to preach what God says in His Word? But God has chosen in the past, and still chooses today, to use weak, inadequate human vessels to communicate His living Word to men. May the dear Lord help us as we give ourselves weekly to sermon preparation. May He bless us as we prepare so that we will indeed be "workmen not ashamed."

Selected Bibliography

Adams, Jay. *Pulpit Speech.* Phillipsburg, N.J.: Presbyterian and Reformed, 1971.

Blackwood, Andrew. *Expository Preaching for Today.* Grand Rapids: Baker, 1943.

———. *Preaching from the Bible.* New York: Abingdon, 1941.

———. *The Preparation of Sermons.* Nashville: Abingdon, 1948.

Brigance, William N. *The Use of Words, Speech, Composition.* New York: F. S. Crofts, 1937.

Broadus, John A. *The Preparation and Delivery of Sermons.* New York: Harper, 1926.

Crandell, S. Judson; Phillips, Gerald M.; and Wigley, Joseph A. *Speech: A Course in Fundamentals.* Glenview, Ill.: Scott Foresman, 1963.

Davis, Benjamin, and Mitchell, Edward C. *Student's Hebrew Lexicon.* Grand Rapids: Zondervan, 1960.

Davis, Henry Grady. *Design for Preaching.* Philadelphia: Fortress, 1958.

Demaray, Donald. *An Introduction to Homiletics.* Grand Rapids: Baker, 1974.

Dickens, Milton. *Speech: Dynamic Communication.* New York: Harcourt Brace Jovanovich, 1954.

Evans, William. *How to Prepare Sermons.* Chicago: Moody, 1964.

Griffen, Emory A. *The Mind Changers.* Wheaton, Ill.: Tyndale, 1976.

Henderson, George. *Lectures to Young Preachers*. Edinburgh: B. McCall Barbour, 1961.

Henderson, George. *The Wonderful Word*. Edinburgh: B. McCall Barbour, n.d.

Horne, Chevis F. *Dynamic Preaching*. Nashville: Broadman, 1983.

Jensen, Irving L. *Enjoy Your Bible*. Chicago: Moody, 1969.

Jones, E. Winston. *Preaching and the Dramatic Arts*. New York: Macmillan, 1948.

Kaiser, Walter C., Jr. *Toward an Exegetical Theology*. Grand Rapids: Baker, 1981.

Koller, Charles W. *Expository Preaching Without Notes*. Grand Rapids: Baker, 1962.

Lloyd-Jones, D. Martyn. *Preaching and Preachers*. Grand Rapids: Zondervan, 1971.

May, Rollo. *The Courage to Create*. New York: Bantam, 1975.

McDowell, Josh. *Syllabus on Communication and Persuasion*. 1983.

McKenzie, E. C. *Mac's Great Book of Quips and Quotes*. Grand Rapids: Baker, 1980.

Meyer, F. B. *Expository Preaching*. Grand Rapids: Baker, 1974.

Overstreet, H. A. *Influencing Human Behavior*. New York: Norton, 1925.

Phillips, John. *One Hundred Sermon Outlines from the New Testament*. Chicago: Moody, 1979.

Prochnow, Herbert. *Speaker's Handbook of Epigrams and Witticisms*. Grand Rapids: Baker, 1955.

Rahskoph, Horace G. *Basic Speech Improvement*. New York: Harper and Row, 1965.

Ray, Jefferson D. *Expository Preaching*. Grand Rapids: Zondervan, 1940.

Riley, W. B. *The Preacher and His Preaching*. Wheaton, Ill.: Sword of The Lord, 1948.

Robinson, Haddon W. *Biblical Preaching*. Grand Rapids: Baker, 1980.

Sarnoff, Dorothy. *Speech Can Change Your Life*. New York: Dell, 1970.

Shannon, Harper. *Trumpets in the Morning*. Nashville: Broadman, 1969.

Spurgeon, C. H. *Lectures to My Students.* London: Marshall, Morgan and Scott, 1954.

Stibbs, Alan. *Expounding God's Word.* Grand Rapids: 1960.

Stott, John R. W. *Between Two Worlds.* Grand Rapids: Eerdmans, 1982.

Thayer, Joseph Henry. *Greek-English Lexicon.* Grand Rapids: Zondervan, 1963.

Unger, Merrill F. *Principles of Expository Preaching.* Grand Rapids: Zondervan, 1955.

Whitesell, Farris D. *Power in Expository Preaching.* Old Tappan, N.J.: Revell, 1963.

Wiersbe, Warren. *Walking with the Giants.* Grand Rapids: Baker, 1976.